If you love something, let it go ...

If you love something, let it go …

Reflections for Ash Wednesday to Pentecost

Charlotte Methuen

British Library Cataloguing in Publication data

A catalogue record for this book is available
from the British Library

ISBN 1 85852 276 5

First published by Inspire
4 John Wesley Road
Werrington
Peterborough PE4 6ZP

Printed and bound in Great Britain by
Stanley L Hunt Printers, Rushden

Dedication

For my Mother
who has sought always
to make her home a house of prayer

Acknowledgements

Scripture Quotations are from the New Revised Standard Version of the Bible, (Anglicized Edition) © 1989, 1995 by the Division of Christian Education of the National Council of the Churches of Christ in the United States of America. Used by permission. All rights reserved.

Contents

Introduction

The reflections in this book began life as sermons preached whilst I was serving as curate and assistant priest in the chaplaincies of the East Netherlands and of Bonn and Cologne in the Church of England's Diocese in Europe, and as Assistant for Reformation History at the University of the Ruhr in Bochum. They reflect my search for a theology which can bring to the hard questions of daily life experienced in a mobile world, where lives take on unexpected directions, futures are often uncertain and even the present is unpredictable, the theological depth and challenge which I encounter in my university work. For, it has always seemed to me, if our theology is not capable of carrying the weight of our most painful concerns whilst retaining its intellectual rigour, then there is something wrong with how we are thinking and talking about God. The shape of the book – Reflections from Ash Wednesday to Pentecost – emerged from my frustration at so often being left hanging by Lent books at (or even before) Easter, with a deep sense that on Easter Sunday the story is not over but, on the contrary, is only just beginning.

In the process that turned unrelated thoughts into sermons and then into this book, I have incurred many debts. First and foremost to the communities in which my preaching has been forged: the people of Arnhem, Nijmegen and Twente in the East Netherlands, of St Boniface, Bonn, of All Saints, Cologne, of the English Church in Heidelberg, and the Parish of Christ the King in Frankfurt-am-Main. My husband, Robert Franke, is one of my best critics. Kevin Franz and Peter Walbrun have been friends and theological sounding-boards along the way. The 'hampers' collected by Hannah Ward and Jennifer

Wild have introduced me to many thoughts and writers, infinitely enriching my preaching. Six weeks at the College of the Transfiguration, Grahamstown in South Africa, offered me not only the stimulating company of the College's students and staff, and of the Anglican Benedictine Community at *uMariya uMama weThemba* Monastery, but time to think and to pray. This book would never have taken shape without the invitation and encouragement of my editor, Natalie Watson. Finally, I am grateful to the 'Thursday Group' in Bonn, Anna Dorst, Devika Homann, Frances Klein, George Williams, Mary Wirths, to Frances Hiller and to Susan Hibbins for their meticulous reading of and comments on earlier drafts.

1

Letting go that we might receive – in preparation

> [Jesus said to his disciples:] 'As the Father has loved me, so I have loved you; abide in my love.'
>
> John 15.9

When I was a teenager I collected posters – as so many teenagers do. I was not very interested in pop stars or footballers, but in horses and animals and neat sayings. One poster that stayed on my wall for a long time showed a seagull flying free, printed over with the words:

> If you love something, let it go.
> If it comes back, it's yours.
> If it doesn't, it never was.

As we move through the seasons of Lent and Easter, these words may help us to make sense of the stories we are telling and hearing, our encounter with the horror of the cross, the joy of the resurrection, the power of Pentecost. Central to the farewell speeches of Jesus to his disciples is Jesus' command: 'Abide in my love!' 'Abide in my love,' Jesus commands his disciples, in his long farewell, in this, John's depiction of Christ's message, written for a community of people who, like us, had themselves never seen the living Jesus. 'Abide in my love!' For John, following this call has something to do with keeping Jesus' commandment to love one other, to lay down our lives for one other; something to do with following Christ in his love and in his sacrifice. Which is to say, with giving up and letting go of what we love.

As we move through Lent, Passiontide and Easter, Ascension and Pentecost, we move through a cycle of letting go and receiving, of giving up in order to be given anew. With the disciples, we come to know Jesus, the man, the companion, his words, his miraculous touch. With them we rejoice as Jesus enters Jerusalem. But then, with them, we must let go of ideas of kingship and revolution. We rejoice at his presence in the city, but then we must let go again, deeply and terribly, must watch Jesus our Christ die in horrible agony on the cross. And yet it is in and through the letting go of Jesus in his passion that the meeting with the resurrected Christ becomes possible. It is that terrible loss and the haunting absence in the tomb which make possible the encounter with the risen Christ in the garden, on the road, in our lives.

Letting go of Jesus whom we love is necessary, for only then can Christ return to us. This is the central movement of the passion and the resurrection. And yet this is not the end of the story. As we approach Ascension, with the disciples we find ourselves preparing once again to let go: of the risen Christ who was Jesus, different and yet the same. After the Ascension, the disciples withdraw, as they did after the crucifixion, to another room, and there they are given the gift of the Holy Spirit, that exhilarating gift of fire and rushing wind – that still small voice – which we celebrate at Pentecost. But that gift, too, could only come to the disciples because they let go of the ascending Christ, of the new way they had come to experience God in the risen Christ: let go of *this* experience of God – in order to receive the presence of God in a different way, in the Holy Spirit. It was in letting go of Christ that they were able most truly to abide in their love of Christ.

This experience of letting go and receiving through Lent and the Easter season reminds us very clearly that the cycle of letting go and receiving is never a 'going back'. The crucified Christ does not return to the disciples as he was before – he is not Jesus, their companion of the road – but is different. The resurrected Christ is not always immediately recognisable. He is glorious, but also wounded and scarred. He is the same but he has changed, and the people to whom he appears have changed. They have been through the terror and the horror of Good Friday. Christ has died in agony on the cross before their eyes. Just as Christ bears the marks of that suffering on his risen body so, too, the disciples carry on their souls the marks of the terrible, lonely pain they have witnessed. In the encounter with the risen Christ, what has been is no longer, and yet all that has been is encompassed: this is still God with them in Christ. To abide in love is to accept this change, to accept the new way that God comes to them, discover Christ anew.

This process of letting go of God, of Christ and of finding ourselves again in God's presence in a different way, is not only the central message of Lent, Holy Week, Easter, Ascension and Pentecost, of the reality of our faith and, indeed, of our whole lives. It is the movement of repentance and new life to which we are called through our baptism. In our life of faith, it will not always be as dramatic as the passion and the resurrection. We enter into it every time we find ourselves tripping over our expectations of how things should be. It might be something as trivial as what kind of landscape makes us joyful (which is not trivial, because this is a question of what feeds our soul). Or something as mundane as our families (who are not mundane, because this is a community in which we experience and live out God's love). Or something as deep as what we truly believe. Letting go in order to receive is about learning to see differently, to let go of how we want things to be, to be open to how things are.

This can be very hard, because the things we love are very important to us, and it can be especially hard when it seems that our identity is bound up in the things we love. Those who experience the dislocation of living in another country know what it is to find that what was obvious where we came from is no longer obvious; what was a part of who we were and how we used to do things can no longer be part of who we have become and how we now do things. Of finding how we have to let go of part of who we were – but are given by the grace of God a way to discover ourselves and our godliness even in that dislocation. Letting go in order to receive. Letting go that we may abide in love.

When I moved to Germany, after years of living in the Peak District and in Scotland, fed by the wild open rugged landscapes there, I felt oppressed and shut in by the forests, cut off from the sky and the wind. On a parish pilgrimage, we walked through beautiful woods – and finally, after years of resenting German forests for not being open Derbyshire hills – I found myself fed by them, appreciating the beauty of what they are, and not simply seeing what they are not. Letting go in order to receive. Letting go that we may abide in love.

'Oh yes,' said a colleague when we spoke about this, 'for me it is my children, and the total disruption they bring into my life, the end of a lot of plans of things I really wanted to do. But what a gift they are, and their love is.' Another friend agonised over her daughter who didn't want to wear fashionable clothes or go to university to study, but was dressed in 'horrible long draggy things', aiming for art school. Until her mother was given the grace to enter into her daughter's plans and to understand what she was trying to do: 'And now I realise what I have been missing,' she said, 'trying to push her into being someone else. She is such a lovely, lovely woman, such a gift to me.' Mundane, and yet the opening of an understanding of God's gift of grace in her daughter. Letting go in order to receive. Letting go in order to abide in love.

Letting go can be particularly hard in the church: for how we have learned to approach God, to worship, to enter into the encounter with Christ is deeply personal, deeply part of who we are in relationship with God. But here, too, we are called to let go: to let old forms and structures die that the gospel may be resurrected.[1] We are called to enter into the realisation that nothing works, that no form of worship can give us a certain encounter with God, to let ourselves risk entering that terrible darkness and to encounter there, in it, the presence and the light of God. 'This brings on a kind of vertigo; it may make me a stranger to my self, to everything that I have ever taken for granted,' writes Rowan Williams.[2] 'If you want God, you must be prepared to let go of all, absolutely all, emotional satisfactions, intellectual and emotional. If you genuinely desire union with the unspeakable love of God, then you must be prepared to have your "religious" world shattered.'[3] As we enter into these depths we let go of what was, in order to discover anew. We let go that we may abide in love.

Letting go in order to discover anew is central to our faith, and to our lives. It turns our expectations upside down. In the prayer attributed to St Francis we pray that in giving we might receive, in dying might enter into eternal life. Letting go that we might receive is not easy. Letting go of Christ, of God, may mean letting go of the security of who God has called us to be, of our certainty about God's call to us, in order to find that calling again. That can be terrible and terrifying. But as we move through Lent, Passiontide, Easter, Ascension, Pentecost, we can and must let go of God. And in the end we will find that, however alone, abandoned, devastated we feel, God does not let go of us. We enter into the depths of pain and grief before crucifixion, into the loneliness of the time after Ascension, into whatever our own dark night is, and in that darkness and that loss, God will be there to meet us: in the risen Christ, in the Holy Spirit, in the person who reaches out to comfort us.

If you love something let it go. If it comes back it's yours. If it doesn't it never was.

If you love God, let God go. God will be with you — because you are God's.

Jesus said: 'As the Father has loved me, so I love you; abide in my love.'

2

Turning towards Christ – Ash Wednesday

The scribes and the Pharisees brought a woman who had been caught in adultery; and making her stand before all of them they said to [Jesus], 'Teacher, this woman was caught in the very act of committing adultery. Now in the law Moses commanded us to stone such women. Now what do you say?' They said this to test him, so that they might have some charge to bring against him. Jesus bent down and wrote with his finger on the ground. When they kept on questioning him, he straightened up and said to them, 'Let anyone among you who is without sin be the first to throw a stone at her.' And once again he bent down and wrote on the ground. When they heard it, they went away, one by one, beginning with the elders; and Jesus was left alone with the woman standing before him. Jesus straightened up and said to her, 'Woman, where are they? Has no one condemned you?' She said, 'No one, sir.' And Jesus said, 'Neither do I condemn you. Go your way, and from now on do not sin again.'

John 8.3-11

The story of the woman taken in adultery offers a stark reminder that none of us is perfect. Here is a group of people who know that they are in the right – but who are challenged by Jesus to examine themselves honestly, and to be clear about where they might be in the wrong. In essence, this is a story about facing up to one's self, about recognising sinfulness and the way of Christ. This is the challenge which each of us faces – consciously or unconsciously

– in our life of faith. And it is a challenge which is particularly present in Lent, as we prepare for Easter.

In the Early Church, baptisms took place at Easter, and Lent was the time when baptismal candidates examined their consciences in preparation for this step that would change their lives. Today, the preparation is not often so intensive, and yet the import of baptism is no less. At baptism and at confirmation in the Church of England, the candidates are asked to answer two sets of three questions. These are questions about orientation: which way are you facing? Which way do you choose?

The questions – and the answers the candidates are required to give – are:

Do you reject the devil and all rebellion against God?
  I reject them.
Do you renounce the deceit and corruption of evil?
  I renounce them.
Do you repent of the sins that separate us from God
    and neighbour?
  I repent of them.
Do you turn to Christ as Saviour?
  I turn to Christ.
Do you submit to Christ as Lord?
  I submit to Christ.
Do you come to Christ, the Way, the Truth and the
    Life?
  I come to Christ.

Many people find this language of rejection, repentance and renunciation difficult. It is important to see that there is a movement implied in these questions, which can perhaps best be seen in the second set. When I turn to Christ, and move towards Christ, then of course I am turning away from all that pulls in the other direction. This is familiar from daily life. If I turn to the left, I turn my back on the right. If I go towards the door, I most likely move away from a window. When I moved to Germany, I left England. The decision to marry this person is – or certainly should be – also a decision not to enter into a certain kind of intimate relationship with a whole lot of other people. Turning towards something, someone, deciding for someone, something, some place, involves letting go, giving up someone else, something, some other place. This is what any commitment is about, including the commitment of faith. When at baptism or confirmation I make the promise to turn to Christ as Saviour, to submit my life to Christ, to come to Christ, the Way, the Truth and the Life, I am making a decision to turn away from those things which pull me in the other direction. I am choosing to reject, renounce, and repent of all which turns me away from Christ, which distracts me from that Way, which calls me into falsehood, which makes my life a living death. In other words, I am making a choice.

Choosing what is of God is not always easy. Indeed, choice itself is not easy. Robert Frost wrote a poem about the difficulty of deciding which path to take: 'Two roads diverged in a yellow wood, / And sorry I could not travel both / And be one traveller, long I stood ....'[1] To the traveller the roads look the same, but he has to choose, and only in retrospect will he discover a reason for his decision, although this was not clear to him at the time: 'Two roads diverged in a wood, and I – / I took the one less travelled by.'

Probably we also recognise Frost's frustration and uncertainty. For the question is, how do we choose? Faced with two options that may be very similar, and knowing we have to choose one of them, it all too often feels as though we simply have no way of knowing how to make the choice, no way of deciding which is of God. We stand at junctions – real or metaphorical – and we weigh up consequences, try to see into the future; and we wonder which we should choose.

The hard thing about choices is that they *are* choices. However attractive each road might look, Frost has to choose one of them. It is simply not possible to half take a job, to be half married, to half have children, to half be a Christian. We may find compromises or creative solutions to some of our dilemmas, but in the end we have to make choices, and live with the consequences of them. The ambiguity of our feelings, which may pull us in more than one direction, has to be resolved with a clarity which may not be at all true to what we feel, and which may even feel frightening. Is the way we have chosen the right way?

On holiday in France several years ago, a friend and I walked long days on paths marked with blobs of paint along the way. In places where the path was well defined, where there was only one way which was well trodden, it was pretty simple to stay on it. Where the blobs of paint followed one after the other there was no doubt about the right way, even if the path didn't seem terribly well worn. And sometimes we were blessed with a clear path, lots of blobs of paint, and the certainty that this was where we were meant to be going. Sometimes life, and life in faith, feels like that. The way is clear, everything drops into place, and the signs are good. Sometimes we can be very sure about our choices and the right way forward.

Sometimes those blobs of paint we were following were not easy to see. Once we followed patches of lichen instead of faded blobs of yellow paint, gradually realising that we were not where we were meant to be. In faith, too, we may mistake the signs, and find that we are on the wrong path.

But there are times when it seems that there are no signs to see, nothing to recognise. On our holiday, on one walk, there was a place where the path we had been following petered out in the middle of a beautiful upland meadow, and there were no blobs of paint in sight. The guidebook we were using was vague, and we could only guess where to go next. Eventually, through a broken-down gateway, we found a sort of path leading over the edge of the cliff and down the side of the gorge to the river, and followed it, knowing that we had to get down to the river somehow. And in the end, but only after we had gone quite a distance along this slight path, there came a blob of paint, and we knew we were going the right way.

Discerning God's intentions is partly a matter of reflecting on our choices, for what we choose takes us on a journey of discovery which is the very essence of our faith. It is on this journey that we become the person that we are, who may or may not be the person that God is calling us to be. Often, it is when we reflect on our choices that we recognise also how we have been drawn away from God, where we have been led astray: our sin. James Alison writes:

> Any non-abstract discussion of sin is for us always the result of some 'aha' moment: 'Oh, so that is what I was doing, and now I see it as falling short of what I am becoming, and must move on, never doing it again, and trying to undo the harm which I did.'[2]

The amazing thing is that any choice, even if – or when – it is one which we later regret, opens up new ways. The glorious truth is that however off track our route takes us, we will find ways – new choices – which lead us back to God. Recently I was in a car with a navigation system and the road we were meant to take was closed. 'Please turn round!' the voice said to us. We drove on. 'Please turn round!' it insisted. But after a while it accepted that we were on a different road and began to give us new directions to reach our goal. Perhaps this is something of what Isaiah means, when he says, 'And when you turn to the right or when you turn to the left, your ears shall hear a word behind you, saying, "This is the way; walk in it" ' (Isaiah 30.21). Even when we go astray, we are never so far astray that we cannot find ourselves once more on the way that leads to God.

Jesus confronts the scribes and the Pharisees who condemn the woman caught in adultery with exactly this kind of 'aha' moment, which jolts them out of their certainty that they are in the right and drives them away. He confronts the woman too. She is not to be condemned, for Christ does not condemn us. But she is to turn away from what she has done and begin anew on the road that leads to God. And so too are we.

> Loving God,
>   you rejoice over all who turn to you.
> Direct our hearts towards you,
>   and give us a new urgency in seeking you,
> that we may live out our faith
>   and do good to others.
> This we ask through Christ,
>   your Son and our Brother,
> who with you and the Holy Spirit
>   is with us and amongst us,
>   now and forever. Amen.[3]

3

With what do we fill our lives? – the first week of Lent

[Jesus said,] 'Why do you call me "Lord, Lord", and do not do what I tell you? I will show you what someone is like who comes to me, hears my words, and acts on them. That one is like a man building a house, who dug deeply and laid the foundation on rock; when a flood arose, the river burst against that house but could not shake it, because it had been well built. But the one who hears and does not act is like a man who built a house on the ground without a foundation. When the river burst against it, immediately it fell, and great was the ruin of that house.'

Luke 6.46-49

Christ calls us to examine our lives, to look at ourselves with honesty and clarity, to determine whether our lives are built securely on rock or insecurely on sand, to discern whether our response 'Lord, Lord' represents a solid response to the calling of Christ, or whether they are empty words. Do our deeds stand up to the light of God, or would we rather hide them away somewhere that God might not look? As we begin to examine our lives in this way, we may well ask the question: with what do we fill our lives?

A professor of philosophy once greeted her class with a glass and a handful of stones. Choosing the biggest stones, she placed them in the glass until no more would fit, and asked the class: 'Is the glass full?' The students replied that it was.

The professor took the glass. One by one, she added to it a handful of much smaller stones, the kind you use to make gravel. They trickled down to fit between the bigger stones. So you see, she said: it was not full before, after all. Is it full now? The students replied, with a little hesitation, that it was.

Out of her briefcase, the professor took a small bag of fine sand. She poured it carefully into the glass. The sand filled the gaps that had been left between the smaller stones, and soon the glass was packed to the top. And now, the class agreed, the glass was really full.

The professor asked the class to think about this as a metaphor for life. The big stones might represent the really important things in life; the smaller stones less important things, and the sand the trivia, fitted in around the bigger things. The point of this picture is not that one can always pack more trivia into one's life. Rather, it reminds us that if the professor had filled the glass with sand first, it would have been full. It would not have been possible to place into it the big stones which represent the really important things; there would have been no room even for the medium-sized stones which represent the fairly important things. It would have been sand, sand, sand, all the way to the top.

In our day-to-day living, it is seductively easy to fill our lives with sand: with the things that seem urgent but are not really important. Too often it takes an upheaval or a catastrophe, a severe illness, or the death of a partner or parent, a child or close friend, the break-up of a relationship, the loss of one's job – an event of that magnitude – to make us stop and reflect, to see whether there is space for the rocks and big stones, for the important aspects, relationships, people. When the crisis comes, then suddenly we realise that other things don't matter, and that the worries that have been filling up our days are, in fact, trivial.

Perhaps such a reflection is possible as well without a crisis. In many ways, separating the stones from the sand, looking at our lives and asking ourselves what is really important to us, is exactly what prayer and repentance are all about. This process is, if you like, a kind of spring-cleaning of our lives, the kind of spring-cleaning which does not just pick up the mess from the floor and shove it unsorted into a cupboard, but which sorts and selects what is to be kept, what is to be thrown away, and what is to be taken to the recycling bin.

This calls for discernment and is not easy. To start with, what is trivia to me may be of enormous importance to others. Nevertheless, it is worth making the effort. For busy people, this can begin with thinking hard about what really makes up that busyness, and what it says about my priorities. Is there time in my life for people or only for tasks? Is there time for the people I care about, or only for the people I have to see? Is there time to appreciate the world, or does it just whizz by outside the car window? Is there time to understand the needs of others, or am I focused on my own survival? Is there time for God, or is this all about me?

Making space for the big things may just mean making space. In an interview, Sir Michael Atiyah, winner of the prestigious Abel Prize for mathematics, explained that he often writes nothing at all in the course of a hard day's work. In maths there are few facts to master, not much reading to be done. 'I just think ... and think.' Atiyah lives with his ideas, carrying them wherever he goes – on a train, a bus, even while asleep – for days, weeks and years, making apparently little discernible progress, but waiting confidently for what he calls 'vision'.[1] In our task-and achievement-oriented world, this is counter-cultural, but it is creative, and it is most likely of God.

The discipline of finding the big rocks and restoring them to their proper place will mean saying no to a good deal of the sand that tends to pack our lives. By doing so, we are taking on the discipline of fasting: 'Any time we say "no" to ourselves we fast,'[2] writes Maggie Ross, whether it is in the sudden surge of standing firm against the temptation of our particular besetting sin (computer games?), or giving up a good option in order to make ourselves available for something of even greater importance. Fasting creates a space and wakes us up to what we really need. 'By temporarily paying less attention to food,' suggests Wayne Simsic, 'we reconnect with a deeper hunger. Instead of being led by desires, we see that we have the freedom to live our lives according to an ultimate sense of truth. Through the ages holy men and women have fasted not because they disliked food or wanted to inflict pain on themselves, but because they wanted to stay connected with the love that they found within.'[3]

Making space for the rocks of importance in our lives may well be to build our house upon the rock. For it allows our lives to be shaped by our true response to God's word and built upon Christ as our sure foundation. This is what Lent is about. In Lent we are called to follow Christ into the desert, there to be confronted with the enormous, essential questions. Lent gives us a liturgical space to reach out beyond the day-to-day questions of how we support our physical existence, of how we are drawn by the seductive attractions of power and status, of how we seek to achieve and to prove ourselves, and to place our trust in the hands of God.

If we use Lent in this way, if we are ready to abandon the fullness of our sand-and trivia-packed lives with their illusions of security and follow Christ into the very different sands of the desert, if we are prepared to seek out rocks of what is essential and build our lives on them, I do not think we should expect comfort. The New Testament scholar Horst Balz once described God as 'dependable but not predictable'.[4] In Lent we open ourselves and our lives to the God upon whom we can depend utterly, but whose actions are often entirely unpredictable.

The discipline of sifting out the big rocks, of opening ourselves to the God upon whom we can depend, is not only fasting, but prayer. It can be uncomfortable, for prayer can be uncomfortable. As Allessandro Pronzato writes, 'Prayer plays havoc on your plans, upsets your itineraries, brings chaos into your ordered life, ruins your arrangements. ... Prayer is confusion, shock, abandonment. You have lost your familiar points of reference. You do not know anything any more. ...'[5] The struggle to discover what is essential in our lives begins with the upheaval of tipping out that glass and sorting out the big stones which act as our foundation. Perhaps it is the experience of 'Things fall apart; the centre cannot hold', as Yeats puts it,[6] for this is when we discover that what we thought was the centre is not.

In our attempts to build our house upon rock, we embark on the road which leads us to the depths of Good Friday and to the heights of Easter. As we travel that road, we will find ourselves, I think, returning again and again to what is essential, to what is before all knowledge and all sense and all explanation: to God, who has mercy on us, in whom we believe and trust.

This my narrow thinking, my distorted view,
    I bring before you now.
Transform me with your wideness.
    Lord, have mercy, please.

This my dreadful weakness,
    that warps and pulls me down,
    I bring before you now.
Transform me with your power.
    Lord, have mercy, please.

This my fearful being, my lost trustfulness,
    I bring before you now.
Transform me with your warm love.
    Lord, have mercy, please.

This my deepest longing for true security,
    I bring before you now.
Transform me with your welcome.
    Lord, have mercy, please.[7]

4

I hate my messy house! – the second week of Lent

Now after John was arrested, Jesus came to Galilee, proclaiming the good news of God, and saying, 'The time is fulfilled and the kingdom of God is come near; repent, and believe in the good news.'

Mark 1.14-15

As we move into the season of repentance, it is worth asking ourselves what repentance is all about. It is a word beloved of caricaturists: 'Repent! The end of the world is nigh!' warns the down-at-heel street evangelist, and we laugh, or shudder, depending on our character or our mood, and go on our way. But do we think of it as a task for ourselves? Perhaps not. Repentance is not very trendy, after all, not a very attractive thought. In any case, what do we have to repent of?

But the call to repentance is not just spoken by weird evangelists on the street. In the words of Mark's Gospel: after he had been tempted 'Jesus came to Galilee proclaiming the good news of God, and saying, "The time is fulfilled, and the kingdom of God has come near; repent, and believe in the good news." '

The Greek word for repentance, *metanoia*, means to change: to change one's opinion, to change one's mind, to change one's life. But originally it meant to know in hindsight, to see differently in retrospect. Writing about repentance, Kathleen Norris tells of a boy who wrote a poem called 'The monster who was sorry':

He began by admitting that he hates it when his father yells at him; his response in the poem is to throw his sister down the stairs, and then to wreck his room, and finally to wreck the whole town. The poem concludes, 'Then I sit in my messy house and say to myself, "I shouldn't have done all that." '[1]

To sit and say, 'I shouldn't have done all that', to recognise that we have done what we ought not to have done, is the beginning of repentance. This is the moment when our eyes open to see the messy house around us, to appreciate the results of our sins of omission and commission: those things which we have done, but that we should not have done; and those things which we have not done, but that we should have done. It is in that realisation that we begin to see the messiness and, in seeing it, feel the need to clear it up. To repent is to open our eyes to see the mess around us, to long to have the messy house tidy, to experience a deep desire to be made clean, and to do something about it.

I am struck by the similarity of the German word for conversion, 'Bekehrung', and the verb to sweep, 'kehren', to sweep. For if repentance is integral to conversion, then perhaps what we are being called to do here is precisely to sweep our messy house clean. As it happens this similarity turns out to be an accident of linguistic history, but the relationship is nonetheless appropriate. The metaphor of setting our house in order, of doing our spiritual sweeping, our spiritual housework, can offer a useful way to approach Lent. For in Lent we are preparing ourselves to receive God, and, as Margaret Guenther writes:

> Guests provide a helpful discipline. Left on
> our own we can walk endlessly round disorder

and uncleanliness, vowing to do something about the state of our house some time, but not now. We may come to love our muddle, to treasure it or at least to take it so for granted that it becomes a comfortable environment. But when an honoured guest is coming, we carry out the rubbish, restore objects to their rightful places, and create an uncluttered, clean and welcoming space.'[2]

The season of Lent is a particular call to this kind of spiritual housework: a spiritual spring-cleaning, if you like. Lent calls us to open the windows on the fusty rooms of our souls, to let light and fresh air into our hearts, to peer into corners that we never touch. It is hard, uncomfortable work: like the little boy sitting in his messy house, surveying the devastation he had effected, we need to see what we have done that we should not have done; to acknowledge where we have acted out of fear, out of defensiveness, out of a desperate wish that things should not be as they are; where we have failed to act out of cowardice, or apathy, or out of comfort. It is hard, uncomfortable work, but God will help us.

In this work of cleaning, as we make ready for God the honoured guest, we are dependent on God's grace. No other person can do this work for us. We may be able to pay (or marry!) someone who will clean our house; we may cajole or coerce someone into picking up our clothes and doing our washing; but we cannot pay anyone else to do the work of cleaning up our souls. This is what the Reformation was about: it began with Luther's objections to the idea that it was possible to buy forgiveness, to pay for conversion, to achieve repentance without change or amelioration of our life. We can't. Repentance calls us to turn ourselves to do God's work; but, in truth, it is

God who gives us the energy and the perseverance to tackle the work at all. God is in charge, wielding the scrubbing brush.

When I was in South Africa, we used sometimes to sing the song of a woman working as a maid in a white woman's house: 'Lord Jesus, come into my soul and scrub, scrub, scrub me clean.' We may make a start at the cleaning, but if our souls are really to be cleansed, it has to be God's work, as in the end Aslan has to strip Eustace of his dragon's skin in C. S. Lewis' *The Voyage of the Dawn Treader*, for Eustace cannot dig deep enough himself.[3]

And when the work is done, it is done not for us, but for God. Just as a clean house is not a showpiece, but a place where people can live, can love (and hate), and think and dream, and laugh and mourn, and offer hospitality, so, too, our soul when it is in readiness for God is not a showpiece – not there so that people will look wonderingly at me – but a place for God to live and work, in us and through us, that others, when they encounter us, may know that they are encountering God too.

One of the things about cleaning the house is that, sadly, it doesn't stay clean. (I have often wondered why God created so much dust.) Spiritually, we are like our houses: our lives, our souls do not remain clean and fresh. Baptism, confirmation, our being washed by the Spirit, do not confer lasting protection against messiness in our souls. On the contrary, through baptism, through the commitment to believe, we enter into a process by which we continually open ourselves to the cleansing power of God's grace, which eradicates that messiness. This is something of what we mean when we talk about original sin: not so much that we are utterly damned from the outset, but that we have a tendency to spiritual grubbiness which cuts us off from the light of God.

When Augustine and Pelagius fell out about original sin, it was partly because Augustine wanted people to realise that they were bound to fall short as Christians again and again. Pelagius wanted people to realise that they couldn't convert to Christianity and carry on living the lives they led before as though nothing had changed: rich Christian Romans should not carry on abusing their power. To Augustine's mind, Pelagius' ideas were dangerous because they left people with the idea that they could live a truly pure or holy life. Augustine knew that they couldn't. He knew that the window panes of our souls get smeared, the corners of our rooms get dusty, that one day we will look up and see that somehow the cobwebs have accumulated again. And having seen the mess, we have to set to again to clean it up, to open the windows of our souls so that God's Spirit can blow in.

Lent is a time for that to happen, to offer hospitality to the cleansing spirit of God. A time for opening the cupboard doors and revealing the messiness we would much rather not know about: the realisation of how dependent we are on that little nibble of chocolate, how difficult it is truly to pray for our divided family, of how much we struggle to make time for God. Light may shine in as positive realisations: how much we enjoy discussing the theme of the Lent group, the discovery that television is not such a hard thing to miss, that less alcohol encourages a sharper focus to our prayers. Whatever we give up or take up should be something to help us to clean up our messy houses and let God in, to help us to see differently, to help us to change, to help us repent.

It is not very exciting work, the elbow-grease of cleaning our spiritual windows and corners. It is not very glamorous. But it is important. Even those who are lucky enough to experience dramatic conversion experiences will find that there is mundane work to be done afterwards. We will find different ways of doing that: patterns of prayer life, reading God's word, experiencing God's presence – in silence, in meditation, in company. It can be tedious, just like housework. But it is necessary and important, because it prepares us to welcome God into our lives.

> Have mercy on me, O God,
>   according to your steadfast love;
> according to your abundant mercy
>   blot out my transgressions.
> Wash me thoroughly from my iniquity,
>   and cleanse me from my sin.
> For I know my transgressions,
>   and my sin is ever before me.
> Against you, you alone, have I sinned,
>   and done what is evil in your sight....
> You desire truth in the inward being;
>   therefore teach me wisdom
>   in my secret heart.
> Purge me with hyssop, and I shall be clean....
> Create in me a clean heart, O God,
>   and put a new and a right spirit within me.
> Do not cast me away from your presence,
>   and do not take your holy spirit from me.
> Restore to me the joy of your salvation,
>   and sustain in me a willing spirit.
>   Psalm 51.1-4a, 6-7a, 10-12

5

Sojourning in a strange land –
the third week of Lent

One sabbath while Jesus was going through
the cornfields, his disciples plucked some heads
of grain, rubbed them in their hands, and ate
them. But some of the Pharisees said, 'Why are
you doing what is not lawful on the sabbath?'
Jesus answered, 'Have you not read what David
did when he and his companions were hungry?
He entered the house of God and took and ate
the bread of the Presence which it is not lawful
for any but the priests to eat, and gave some to
his companions?' Then he said to them, 'The
Son of Man is lord of the sabbath.'

Luke 6.1-5

As we open ourselves to God, we begin to struggle
with what it means to be God's people in the world.
There are different models for this, many of which see
the world as the enemy of the holy. Their assumption
is that the ways of the world, the priorities that the
world may take for granted, the accepted ways of
doing things, the normality in which we live, all of
these things cannot be assumed to be acceptable to
God. God's ways, God's Spirit, God's priorities are all
different.

But the stories of Jesus and the sabbath give us
another picture. Here we find a reminder that
religion must be aware of the needs of the world; that
it must not forget the world. The rules of religion do
not determine how God works, but instead, 'the Son
of Man is lord of the sabbath'. There seems here to be
a strong implication that God and the world are not
enemies.

Sometimes, radical action may be necessary to stand up for God's ways, for God's priorities. Intervention may be necessary. We may be called to confess what we believe. We all know of situations in which people have felt that they must make a stand. We might think, for example, of Dietrich Bonhoeffer of Martin Luther King, or of Edith Stein, and their obstinate refusal to give way to injustice. We may know of situations in our own lives: perhaps we have been confronted with deep dishonesty at work. There are situations in which our faith calls us to take a radical stand, in which it is obvious that our faith calls us to different priorities.

It may be tempting to make that a permanent way of being: the Church against the wicked corruption of the world; the battling band of soldiers; Christ and the Christians safe inside the ark sailing the waters of the flood. One way of dealing with differences is to shut ourselves away in a safe place and simply stay there. It can be tempting to seek to surround ourselves with purity, to cleanse our community of what we think God sees as wickedness and dirty dealing, and to leave the world to go its own corrupt way. But surely that is not what faith in God is really about? Christ mixed with tax-collectors, sinners, adulterers and hypocrites. Christ was sent into the world, although he did not belong to the world. And Christ sends us into the world in just the same way that he was sent into the world (John 17.16-18), to be the salt of the earth, the light on the hill (Matthew 5.13-16). We are called to be salt and light, that the world may taste and see that the world is good (Psalm 34.8a). We may not belong to the world, but we cannot simply cut ourselves off from it.

For however much we would prefer to be a safe, closed community – and however hard we may try to create one – we are inevitably, irredeemably, in the world and called to preach its redemption. That reality touches our lives as Christians at a very basic level. We know that because we are constantly confronted by dilemmas in our lives. What is honest here? Whom should I tell what? How do I deal with the knowledge that if I encourage this development – good for the firm – other people's jobs will be at stake? What do I do when I find out that two people I care about are deceiving each other? Do I smack my child? Or, on a larger scale: what can I do about the terrible poverty in the world? Precisely because we are called to witness to Christ, we can never distance ourselves so completely from the world that these dilemmas do not impinge.

These dilemmas are not new. The author of 1 John knows them too, and phrases the problem in terms of different sorts of spirit:

> Do not believe every spirit, but test the spirits to see whether they are from God ... Little children, you are from God, and have conquered [the spirits from the world]; for the one who is in you is greater than the one who is in the world. They are from the world; therefore what they say is from the world, and the world listens to them. We are from God. Whoever knows God listens to us, and whoever is not from God does not listen to us. From this we know the spirit of truth and the spirit of error.
>
> 1 John 4.1, 4-6

Here the author is making a clear distinction between the spirits which are of the world and those which are of God. We know which is which, because 'whoever knows God listens to us, and whoever is not from God does not listen to us'. This could be interpreted in terms of understanding: those who come from God understand each other; and so do those who come from the world. It is almost as though the spirits are speaking different languages: the language of the world and the language of God.

It can indeed be helpful, when we think about the Church and the world, about the Spirit of God and the spirit of falsehood, about Christ and Anti-Christ, to think along the lines of different languages. For it means that when we think about being the Church in the world, there is a sense in which we are thinking about living at the boundary between two cultures, at the point at which two languages meet. As Christians we are called to live out our faith in a world that does not share the values which we identify as Christian. That is, as Christians we live as people in a foreign country have to do: we make our home in a land, a language and a culture which is and remains in some ways strange.

People who live across different cultures know about the questioning, tensions and compromises that this entails. Attitudes, ideas, customs that the country or culture of origin took for granted are greeted as strange, or odd, radical or incredibly conservative; value systems simply don't fit. People are daily confronted with questions of identity: who am I when I am in a strange land? Who do I become when I speak a different language? As they settle into a new country, people learn the language, but they also make choices, accepting some new ideas and rejecting others. Expectations change. Normality looks different. Everybody who lives abroad, even those who live in 'ex-pat' or well-defined cultural communities, is affected by their environment. They may seek solace with others who speak their own language, or with others who are going through the same experience. But they still learn and change. When they return to the countries or communities that they came from, they discover that they have been shaped by their experiences and encounters. Parts of who they are will have been confirmed by being exposed to different expectations or patterns of living; other parts of them will have been changed.

Living in a foreign country is not only about negative experiences, not only about defensiveness, fighting things off, but also- and often primarily- about opening and growing and changing. It is about how people discern what they can accept, what they can become and what they can't. All of us live amongst, and deal with, constantly shifting priorities and attitudes and values, but those who exist at the cusp between two cultures and two languages are perhaps especially aware of that.

As Christians we do this too. We cannot shut ourselves off from the influence of the world, and if we seek to do so we are missing out on the possibility of enrichment. What we learn in our daily lives, the people we encounter, the issues we face, may offer huge challenges to what we believe. Sometimes we may indeed have to make a radical stand, to throw out the money-changers, or build an ark and sail away. Sometimes we may be faced with the need to make a difficult compromise. And sometimes we may learn and benefit from what we are offered, from the changes in perspective. Community is important here; meeting with others, sharing, talking our own language, without having to explain ourselves, is essential. But so, too, is the mutuality in which we live. Much of what we learn and encounter in our lives enriches us as people of faith, and in doing so it enriches the way in which we are able to be Christ's body in the world.

O God, you loving friend of humankind,
you sent Jesus into the world
to seek out all those who were lost
and to gather in
   all those who had been rejected.
Be with us through all the ways of our life,
and bring us always back to you,
the source of eternal life.
To whom be all honour and glory,
   through Jesus Christ, your Son,
in the Holy Spirit, for ever and ever.
Amen.[1]

6

The depths of depression – the fourth week of Lent

My God, my God, why have you forsaken me? Why are you so far from helping me, from the words of my groaning? O my God, I cry by day, but you do not answer; and by night, but find no rest. … I am poured out like water, and all my bones are out of joint; my heart is like wax; it is melted within my breast; my mouth is dried up like a potsherd, and my tongue sticks to my jaws; you lay me in the dust of death.

Psalm 22.1-2, 14-15

As we seek our identity in faith, opening ourselves to become the person who God is calling into being, most of us have times when we feel 'un-called', left alone, exhausted and dry, cut off from God. The journey of faith will almost inevitably bring us to the terrible experience, described by the psalmist, of feeling ourselves utterly cut off from God. 'My God, my God, why have you forsaken me?' These were Christ's words on the cross. Perhaps this is what Margaret Silf describes as 'that inner howling that comes from the deep awareness of something wrong, that no amount of theology is going to cure for us!'[1] In this moment we may find ourselves standing at the foot of the cross, or know ourselves crucified with Christ in our agony and our despair. Or we may just have a sense of being somehow absent ourselves, of hearing the calls and promises of faith as if from a distance, of seeing the promises of God as though through opaque glass. These are the times, as R.S. Thomas puts it, 'When a black frost is on / One's whole being, and the heart / In its bone belfry hangs and is dumb.'[2]

These are the times, too, when the words of the life of faith, promises of eternal life, of life and prayer in the Spirit, of the love of God, feel empty; when we hear the call to 'taste and see that the Lord is good', and can't be bothered, partly because we know that if we were to taste, our mouths would be filled with some kind of eternal sawdust, and if we were to see, our eyes would capture only grey emptiness. Any idea of being filled with the Spirit seems nonsensical, and joyful songs sung unto the Lord seem like the dreadful cacophony of so many trumpets. Faith – and with it life – can be hard, not so much because it is challenging, but because we simply can't engage. Nothing seems to matter, and nothing seems to make sense.

Depression is what we call these feelings today, but they have been around for a lot longer than that particular term. 'Accidie', it has been called, listlessness, torpor. John of the Cross called these feelings 'the dark night of the soul', the experience of distance from God, distance from life, distance from meaning. Although in these times we may feel far away from God, such experiences of distance have given rise to some of the deepest writing and thinking about God. The experience is common to us all. None of us sails through life without being touched by doubt, without ever experiencing the aridity of not being able to hear God, without ever having phases of feeling that nothing makes any sense.

This is important to realise because part of the dark night – our own, personal dark night – can be a feeling of utter aloneness. The knowledge that the experience is shared, that in the experience of the dark night we are not alone, will not take it away, although knowing that others are vulnerable too – that everyone is vulnerable, not just me – may help to make my particular darkness more bearable. Knowing that this is part of the journey for everyone may give us the courage to admit that it is happening. 'The world is not divided into the strong who care and the weak who are cared for. We must each in turn care and be cared for, not just because it is good for us, but because that is the way things are,' writes Sheila Cassidy, a doctor who specialises in hospice work and who is herself prone to depression.[3]

In the loneliness of pain and darkness it is possible to become very selfish, focused only on ourselves. The first step out of that can be the recognition that others share our own vulnerabilities; that we can meet others in our darkness, who share, not our particular pain, but pain; who have their own experiences, their own struggles, their own times of nothingness. Community is important: a community in which we can take the risk of sharing with one another in truth: not just our joys but our griefs, not just our times of being full of life, but our times of meaningless and torpor.

But there is more: there is the discipline of our spiritual life. R.S. Thomas was certainly no stranger to dark times. But even in those times of darkness, he writes of the importance of knowing that others at least were praying:

> Always,
> Even in winter in the cold
> Of a stone church, on his knees
> Someone is praying, whose prayers fall
> Steadily through the hard spell
> Of weather that is between God
> And himself.[4]

Even when it seems meaningless, even when we feel cut off from God by fog or storm, we are called to the discipline of prayer. That may mean different things for different people. For some it will mean regular times alone with the Bible, a pattern of morning prayer, a project of reading, regular times of silence, of reflection, in church. Making time for God in this kind of spiritual discipline is both 'our duty and our joy' as the Church of England's eucharistic liturgy puts it, recognising that we are not always going to sing glad hymns to the Lord, but that we are still bound to give thanks. I think this is something of what Paul means when he calls Christians in Ephesus to put on the armour of God. The discipline can help us not to sink into whatever our own personal temptation is: dulling the pain with overwork, or wine, or drugs, or excessive shopping, or obsessive computer games, reading trashy novels, or whatever it is that we use to fill up those empty times and to numb the aching emptiness.

Of course, we should not expect miracles: our practise of spirituality reflects how we feel; it cannot simply transform the way we are currently seeing the world. In our dark times, the time we take consciously to be with God may seem as empty and pointless as all the rest: much more a duty than a joy, perhaps even painful, because the emptiness points particularly to the distance we feel from God, shows up the pitiful inadequacy of our prayer. But even if these spiritual times are times during which we feel nothing but distance, that in itself is truth: that feeling may be the beginning of feeling an anguish of God's absence, of a thirst for God, a thirst for meaning, and that may in turn be the beginning of a new search for meaning, a new encounter with God's own self.

The Scottish reformer John Knox once wrote to his sister-in-law that her anxiety and anguish about having lost any sense of having a relationship to God meant at the very least that she had a sense that God should be there. And that, he wrote, is infinitely better than not caring at all. Our very sense that God has somehow withdrawn, that there is an absence where there should be a presence, may become our understanding of how God is present at this time. 'My God, my God, why have you forsaken me?' groans Christ on the cross, at the point where God is most present in the sufferings of humankind, in the person of his Son. And if we in truth and honesty can groan that too, then we may find, as R.S. Thomas seems to have done, that even in the dark times our prayers, our times of opening ourselves to God, may indeed become 'warm rain / That brings the sun and afterwards the flowers / On the raw graves and throbbing of bells'.[5]

In discovering who and where we are and how we are trapped, and shut away from God, we may also begin to see how God is with us. Margaret Silf writes of walking by a canal and watching a narrow boat in a lock:

> I realised that I myself feel rather like a narrow boat in the lock chamber with the lock gates firmly closed on me. ... It often feels as though I am here in a deep, dark prison facing brick walls on every side, and with no way out that my mind can guess at or imagine. A pointless and a daunting place to be. If I think about my condition at all, I start to examine every brick or stone in that lock chamber, as if it were the whole arena of my living, and in the hope that a minute examination of its walls might reveal some meaning in it, or some way of dealing with it.

This process of examining my prison walls, though it may be absorbing, is ultimately rather futile, because it completely lacks perspective. The lock chamber makes no sense at all unless you know about the canal. Without the canal, the boat is truly just a prisoner in a pointless place. But when the reality of the canal is felt and embraced, *then* the transformation happens. Then the lock chamber is seen to be the place, and the *only* place, where God's grace might be inflowing, to raise me to the place where I must be.[6]

As we journey through the wilderness of Lent through the Passion to meet the risen Christ, to open ourselves to the Holy Spirit, let us pray that God may take the place where we are – however dark, however dank – and use it to bring us closer to God.

The Lord is my shepherd, I shall not want.
He makes me lie down in green pastures;
     he leads me beside still waters;
     he restores my soul.
He leads me in right paths for his name's sake.
Even though I walk through the darkest valley,
     I fear no evil,
     for you are with me;
     your rod and your staff – they comfort me.
You prepare a table before me
     in the presence of my enemies;
you anoint my head with oil;
     my cup overflows.
Surely goodness and mercy shall follow me
     all the days of my life,
and I shall dwell in the house of the Lord
     my whole life long.

Psalm 23

7

If your hand sins, cut it off –
the fifth week of Lent

[Jesus said,] 'If your hand causes you to stumble, cut it off; it is better for you to enter life maimed than to have two hands and to go to hell, to the unquenchable fire. And if your foot causes you to stumble, cut it off; it is better for you to enter life lame than to have two feet and to be thrown into hell. And if your eye causes you to stumble, tear it out; it is better for you to enter the kingdom of God with one eye than to have two eyes and to be thrown into hell.'

Mark 9.43-47

Here is a text which seems entirely opposed to our modern way of thinking. There is nothing here of accepting ourselves as we are, warts and all, nothing of coming to terms with the parts of us which we don't much like. This is far more radical: if your hand offends you, cut it off. If your foot causes you to stumble, hack it off. If your eye causes you to sin, tear it out. If it does wrong, get rid of it! This is a simple (perhaps it seems even simplistic?), radical call for exorcism, a call for the excising of the instruments of sin, on the assumption that if the instrument is gone, the cause is gone too. Or is it?

I'm not sure. This passage was certainly intended to shock. It is saying something very radical about how we are to follow the gospel, but I don't think that it is actually a call to physical self-mutilation. Nor is its message as simple – or as simplistic – as 'if you get rid of the instrument, you get rid of the cause'. In fact, it does not seem to me that this passage is about judgement or punishment of others at all. Instead it calls me to look at my own behaviour, to examine myself with deep and devastating honesty: if your hand causes you to stumble, cut it off: not if her or his hand commits what you think is a sin, cut if off for them! This is certainly not a passport to judge the behaviour of others, but rather a demand that, if I am going to judge anybody, I must judge myself.

The crux of what Jesus is saying seems to me to be in the conclusions he draws: 'It is better for you to enter life maimed than to have two hands, two feet, two eyes, and go to hell.' He is speaking to a people who probably understood physical health and a perfect body to be a sign of God's blessing, and he is wanting to jolt them. And so he turns their expectations on their heads, saying: it is better to be maimed – that is, it is better to bear what are apparently the outward signs of God's displeasure – but to live in God's grace, than to *look* blessed but be on the road to hell. Life in Christ, eternal life, life rooted in faith and the love of God, is more important than having two hands, two feet, two eyes, a healthy body, or than any outward appearance.

Put like that, perhaps it is easier to recognise ourselves and our own lives. For we probably know people whose lives are apparently ordered, outwardly wonderful, but who have some sort of a cancer eating away at the centre of their being. What of those comfortable looking families where the husband batters his wife? Or the neighbours who 'always looked so nice' – until the fraud squad caught up with them? Or the person whose tidy house conceals the empty bottles of the alcoholic behind the polished doors? Or the supposedly happy marriage where one partner is deeply, desperately depressed? Or the family which is living a lie of good health while one person in it is dying? Or, indeed, the affluent society which hides its poor round the corner, in another part of town? There are people in our society who do indeed have two hands, two feet, two eyes, whose lives look outwardly perfect, but who nonetheless find themselves treading the road to some kind of hell.

As we move into Passiontide, perhaps we need to understand that dark centre in each of us, the dark centre which drove those who betrayed Jesus Christ and sent him to trial and to his death. Perhaps we need to look at ourselves with honesty, seeking to admit and face whatever is the heart of the darkness in our own souls. For it is in admitting that it is there, that we are able to confess to one another and pray for one another that we might be healed (James 5.16). For we all need that healing; we all need forgiveness; we all need God's love. The Church is a school for sinners, not a society for saints. As God's chosen people, we are a community of the forgiven, of those who have sinned, have been forgiven, and who will doubtless sin again. We are God's people, God's chosen people, precisely because we are not whole, because we are broken, sinful people. We turn to Christ, not because we are whole, because we have two hands, two feet and two eyes, but because we know in our heart of hearts that there is something deeply wrong with one of our hands, with our vision, with the way we walk. We come to Christ because, knowing that, we know, too, how much we need God's grace, God's forgiveness. And when we turn to Christ, we may find ourselves facing a radical and even terrifying break with what we have been until now.

The Scripture that calls us to tear out the parts of us that cause us to sin also warns us, 'It is a fearful thing to fall into the hands of the living God'

(Hebrews 10.31). Faith is not a matter of an easy life; the good news is not a sugary romance; conversion is not followed by an eternal, rosy glow of satisfaction. Instead, faith involves the recognition that tribulation precedes vindication; that the encounter with God is an encounter with a fierce beauty, with a refining fire, with the terror and fearsomeness and awe of God.

In the Gospel of Mark, and for the author of Hebrews, the talk of suffering, of persecution, of the fearfulness of falling – or putting oneself – into the hands of the living God says something very important about the cost of discipleship, about the sacrifice involved in following Christ on the way of the cross. And, although in our lives we may not be confronted by explicit persecution, we too are faced with life-changing situations of testing and of pain and fear, which expose us to ourselves, and which may leave us shamed by our inadequacy and overwhelmed by circumstances. Joan Puls calls such experiences 'radicalizing experiences':

> Radicalizing experiences, that is, moments of risk, plunge us into deeper waters than we currently know. All of us accept the importance of such moments in the life of every human being. Bearing a child, undergoing surgery, losing a loved one, necessary separations, marriage itself, require risk and upset our usual routine and patterns ... [leaving] unforgettable markings on my spirit, unseasoned and overprotected. Such are the effects of entering radically different realms, realms that open our eyes, jar our habitual mindsets and values and force us to re-evaluate our attitudes and our actions. They put into the balance what is familiar and acceptable and challenge us to go deeper, to enlarge our narrow ideas and our reluctant hearts. We are never again quite the

same. We lose some of our complacency and we are humbled by our inability to adapt and our limited understanding of life. We are also forever opened to further risk and further adventures. Radicalizing experiences are baptisms of the spirit, preparation for living in new ways.[1]

Baptism is the beginning, not of safety, but of risk, of danger, of tearing out the parts of us that are not of God. That is, indeed, the fearful – fearsome – experience of finding ourselves in the hands of the living God. Baptism opens us up to the experience of what Dietrich Bonhoeffer called costly grace:

> This grace is costly, because it calls us to discipleship; it is grace, because it calls us to be disciples of Jesus Christ. It is costly, because it costs people their lives; it is grace because it grants them true life. It is costly, because it condemns sins; it is grace because it justifies the sinner. This grace is costly above all because it was costly to God, because it cost God the life of his son ... and because something that cost God so much cannot be cheap to us. But this grace is grace above all because for God the gift of his son was not too costly for our life. Costly grace is the incarnation of God.[2]

It is costly grace, costly forgiveness because it does not leave us undisturbed, convicted of our own rightness. It touches us deeply; it converts and changes us; it takes us and turns us around. When we have been touched by God, those certainties we relied on, those hands, and feet and eyes, those outward signs, those worldly weights and measures, suddenly won't support us any more. And when we find that, I think, we will also find that we have, indeed, cast out that hand, that foot, that eye; we will discover that we are touching God's world and moving amongst God's people and seeing the light of God's love quite differently. And therein we may recognise the harrowing, excising touch of God's grace.

> God is our refuge and strength,
>   a very present help in trouble.
> Therefore we will not fear,
>   though the earth be moved,
> though the mountains shake
>   in the heart of the sea;
> though its waters roar and foam,
> though the mountains tremble with its tumult.
>
> Psalm 46.1-3

8

Take up your cross – Passiontide

Once when Jesus was praying alone, with only the disciples near him, he asked them, 'Who do the crowds say that I am?' They answered, 'John the Baptist; but others, Elijah; and still others, that one of the ancient prophets has arisen.' He said to them, 'But who do you say that I am?' Peter answered, 'The Messiah of God.' He sternly ordered and commanded them not to tell anyone, saying, 'The Son of Man must undergo great suffering, and be rejected by the elders, chief priests and scribes, and be killed, and on the third day be raised.'

Then he said to them all, 'If any want to become my followers, let them deny themselves and take up their cross daily and follow me. For those who want to save their life will lose it, and those who lose their life for my sake will save it. What does it profit them if they gain the whole world, but lose or forfeit themselves?'

Luke 9.18-25

As we draw closer to the moments of betrayal, of crucifixion and of death, we draw closer to sacrifice and to suffering. Sacrifice and suffering are not themes which have much credibility in our society. But in the words of Christ to his disciples, we have both the clear statement of what is to happen to him – that before he is raised, the Son of Man is to suffer, to be rejected, and to die – and a clear call to all who want to follow him: 'Take up your cross; be prepared to give up your life!' In Lent we hear again and again this message of sacrifice, of submission. 'The sacrifice acceptable to God is a broken spirit; a broken and contrite heart, O God, you will not despise' (Psalm 51.17). The way of faith is the way of the cross: sacrifice; suffering; denial.

It is a small step from the stark realisation that faith requires sacrifice to the false conclusion that the essence of faith must be suffering. And in making that false step, it is easy – to my mind misleadingly easy – to make another: to turn this around and to suggest that those who suffer must necessarily be those who are believing properly. It is then an even smaller step to move on and argue that true faith requires uncomplaining, unresisting suffering. This is dangerous, for it accepts unquestioningly that all suffering is of God. It turns quickly into the mentality that sends brutally beaten women back to their violent husbands in the name of God, or that offers those living in abject poverty no more than the uplifting thought that what they are enduring is good for their souls. It is an attitude which comes dangerously close to equating sacrifice automatically with victim. And this is wrong, for the call to take up my cross and follow Christ, the exhortation that I should lose my life for Christ's sake, is not a call to be a victim.

The way of the cross offers no trite equation of faith and sacrifice and suffering. Christ is not making a bargain with us, is not setting out to measure what sacrifice we are prepared to make, how much pain we are prepared to bear. To say, or to think, 'I only believe right when I am hurting' or, even worse, 'If I am hurting it must be a sign that I have things right' is too simplistic, for it puts the suffering first, the sacrifice before the faith, and leads quickly to an unhealthy, somewhat masochistic self-righteousness.

The theologians of the Early Church had some hard words to say about those who sought martyrdom, because seeking martyrdom, suffering, sacrifice can very soon become a glorification of suffering, of hurt or of pain, and, indeed, a glorification of self. 'Look at me! I am so good because I have it so bad!' Christ's call to us to take up our cross is not a glorification of suffering for its own sake, but straight talking: if we want to follow his way, to walk where he has walked, then we are not always going to have it easy. It is a message which we encounter again and again in Luke's Gospel. Only those who hate their mother and their father, their brother and their sister, who give up all their possessions, who carry their cross, who give up even life itself, are in truth the disciples of Christ (Luke 14.26, 27, 33). If we choose the way of Christ, we should know what to expect: conflict with our families, loss of possessions, abandonment of all that we had previously taken for granted. 'Take up my cross!'

The point here is precisely *not* that we should seek out suffering and sacrifice in order to walk the way of Christ but that, as we go Christ's way, they will seek us. Although theologians of the Early Church condemned those who sought martyrdom, they also had some hard words to say about those who denied their faith and ran away from martyrdom. Our faith also may call us into situations of suffering and sacrifice which we cannot avoid.

In the story of the binding of Isaac, it seems to me that Abraham faces this kind of choice. He is confronted with some kind of impossible decision between his love for his son and his respect for his God. Two deeply important facets of himself come into conflict. And it is that conflict which is expressed in this radical, horribly graphic story: Abraham takes his son to the place of sacrifice and builds the fire and sharpens the knife, and yet is saved at the last moment from killing his son. Abraham is lucky, for his appalling choice turns out to be theoretical. Even so, as Sara Maitland has suggested, Abraham may well have found that the consequences were terrible beyond his worst expectations. In a short story, she explores the destruction of the family which she imagines followed from Abraham's readiness to sacrifice of Isaac. Nothing can relieve the appalling fear with which Isaac regards his father: his father who was prepared to give him up to death. His son is now terrified of him, and his wife cannot speak to him:

> It was not that she could not forgive him, or even that she could not forgive herself. It was that she had nothing to say to a man who believed that God had blessed him for being willing to kill her child.[1]

In Sara Maitland's story, Abraham's step of faith has torn the family apart, putting husband and wife on different sides of a boundary of faith. Sarah cannot comprehend how Abraham could possibly believe his actions to be obedience to God; Abraham cannot believe that this is not of God.

We too are, or can be, faced with agonising choices and situations in our lives, with choices which mean that we have to give something up, or with situations which confront us with sacrificing the very core of what we are. It may not be immediately obvious that the difficult decisions with which we are confronted are of God or have to do with our faith. Perhaps a relationship is in difficulty. I am faced with the decision between leaving, and causing enormous hurt to someone I love, or remaining, with the horrible sense that something in me is being destroyed.

Perhaps there is a job offer that will keep the family from financial ruin, but will uproot them from where they are happy and settled and take them to a strange place or a foreign country. Or the heart-rending decision of whether to terminate a pregnancy, when the parents know that the baby is disabled. The tearing struggle between what our integrity calls us to deny and what people in authority tell us is right. Perhaps we find ourselves coming to the horrible realisation that something or someone we really care about seems to be holding us back from coming closer to God. We can all find ourselves in situations in which whatever course of action we choose seems destined to cause enormous hurt and damage to somebody else. It is in and through such situations that we begin to understand the meaning of sacrifice, of giving up our lives, of becoming disciples of Christ.

Such situations are not sacrifice sought out for sacrifice's sake. They are not a self-inflicted, self-righteous martyrdom. The fearful reality of faith is discovered in how we live through them. As a consequence of his strivings for justice and racial equality in the American South, Martin Luther King experienced detention, bombings and death threats. He reflected:

> As my sufferings mounted I soon realised that there were two ways in which I could respond to my situation – either to react with bitterness or seek to transform the suffering into a creative force. I decided to follow the latter course. Recognizing the necessity for suffering, I have tried to make of it a virtue. If only to save myself from bitterness, I have attempted to see my personal ordeals as an opportunity to transfigure myself and heal the people involved in the tragic situation which now obtains. I have lived these last few years

with the conviction that unearned suffering can be redemptive.[2]

True sacrifice is redemptive. And true sacrifice comes about when a decision – perhaps a decision taken fairly casually – has brought us to this place we would really prefer not to be. Rowan Williams once wrote in the voice of the apostle Peter at the fire after the trial of Jesus: 'I never knew that healing a leper or sharing a meal with a prostitute might cost you a life.'[3] Peter, who denied his Lord, and then had to live with the shattering guilt of that denial. Abraham could probably have said the same thing: 'I did not know that following my God could bring me to risk my son to the point of death.' And so might we: 'I did not know that the stakes were so high.' 'I did not know that faith could require of me something so drastic that I would find myself living with the consequences for years to come.' 'I did not know that faith could cost me my life.'

And yet:

'If any want to become my followers, let them deny themselves and take up their cross daily and follow me. For those who want to save their life will lose it, and those who lose their life for my sake will save it. What does it profit them if they gain the whole world, but lose or forfeit themselves?'

Luke 9.23-25

9

Rocking the foundations – Palm Sunday

[The disciples] brought the donkey and the colt, and put their cloaks on them, and [Jesus] sat on them. A very large crowd spread their cloaks on the road, and others cut branches from the trees and spread them on the road. The crowds that went ahead of him and that followed were shouting, 'Hosanna to the Son of David! Blessed is the one who comes in the name of the Lord! Hosanna in the highest heaven!' When he entered Jerusalem, the whole city was in turmoil, asking, 'Who is this?' The crowds were saying, 'This is the prophet Jesus from Nazareth in Galilee.' Then Jesus entered the temple and drove out all who were selling and buying in the temple, and he overturned the tables of the money-changers and the seats of those who sold doves. He said to them, 'It is written, "My house shall be called a house of prayer"; but you are making it a den of robbers.' The blind and the lame came to him in the temple, and he cured them. But when the chief priests and the scribes saw the amazing things that he did, and heard the children crying out in the temple, 'Hosanna to the Son of David', they became angry.

Matthew 21.7-15

Palm Sunday: the joy and excitement of Jesus' arrival in Jerusalem. The exuberance, the shouting crowds, the waving palm leaves, the celebration. The party. Jesus the Messiah has arrived! Hosanna to the Son of David!

Being swept away on a tide of joy and excitement – it happens. It can happen to anyone. It can and does – and should – happen to all of us that we experience great joy, the wish to celebrate. Perhaps we are swept away on the tide of love. Or consumed with delight over that long-awaited job. Or finally pregnant after years of hoping for a child. Or caught up in the excitement of coming to faith. Times to celebrate. Hosanna to the Son of David! Let's welcome him with palm branches, with the coats off our backs. Let's throw a party! Let's praise the coming of the Messiah; ride off into the sunset, fly high on the cloud of champagne; let us be swept up in the excitement of a new love.

If the gospels were a film, surely they would end here, at the fairy-tale ending: this seems to be the way it should be. Here we have the Messiah, the Saviour long-expected by the Jews, arriving in his own city, approaching his own temple, fulfilling the Old Testament prophecies. The Messiah come into his own, accepted by his own. The cause won. This, we might think, is the point at which all is fulfilled. The perfect end to an exciting story. Everything the way it should be.

But we know that the story does not end here. We know that this joyful excitement, the acceptance of Jesus, is going to turn sour. We know that the joy and jubilation of Palm Sunday does not last. The joy turns to pain, the jubilation to anger and betrayal. The cries of welcome to the Son of David will turn to demands for his death, to shouts of 'Crucify him!' These crowds who are shouting that Jesus is Lord, who are welcoming the Messiah into Jerusalem, are precisely the same people who will turn against him, who will reject what he has to offer.

The events of Holy Week, which follow Palm Sunday, remind us at the very deepest level of what our faith requires of us. If we allow them to, the events of Holy Week will confront us with our own expectations of faith, our own hopes in faith, our fears and our doubts; show us where we have had faith in our own structures instead of in God. For this great celebration, which turns into deep rejection, has parallels in our lives and in our faith. The gospel of love that turns to hate. The loving relationship that ends in confrontation. The job that eats us away inside. The much-wanted child who keeps us awake at night. All these can drive us to distraction, to rejection, even to violence.

It may be tempting to watch the events of Palm Sunday and the betrayals that follow with a kind of detached superiority. We may find ourselves looking at them as evidence that the Jewish people didn't really know what sort of messiah they were looking for. We may observe this joyful crowd which will so soon condemn Jesus, and reflect how weak their faith seems to be. Here they are, celebrating the arrival of Jesus, but just one suggestion by the Pharisees later and they've changed their minds, switched to the other side, and are calling for Jesus' death. 'They're not much use, are they?' we may think, comfortably.

But if we see the crowd as made up of people like ourselves, we may well wonder if we too might not have reacted in much the same way. Surely these people who celebrate the coming of Jesus the Messiah are good believers. They are people like you and me, who have worked out ways which help them to find God and who seek to live out their faith. They are people who go to the temple, who find comfort in difficult times by buying doves for sacrifice. (And is it so bad if a service industry has developed at the

Temple, to satisfy their needs, to sell doves and to make money to keep the Temple afloat, all done to the glory of God?) These are people who believe strongly in the Messiah, who are carried and sustained and uplifted by that hope.

Hopes breed expectations, and expectations can be disappointed. The people in this crowd did not just hope for the Messiah. They believed deeply and desperately in the liberation he would bring. They were an oppressed people; their city was occupied by the Romans; they knew what kind of freedom the Messiah would bring. And here he was! And so they rejoiced: 'Hosanna to the Son of David!'

Now everything should get easier. But it doesn't. Only a few days later, the devout seller of doves, who was perhaps there cheering with the crowd, has his table turned over in the Temple, loses his livelihood, realises that this Christ is coming to change things – including his faith.

Do we expect somehow that faith, the search for God, the encounter with Jesus Christ will iron out all our troubles? A theological student in the Democratic Republic of the Congo once said to me: 'I thought that when I became a Christian everything would get easier, that I wouldn't suffer any more.' Do we somehow have this expectation too? Are we pinning our hopes on a God who will take all our troubles away? Do we expect faith to be a kind of magic wand to conjure away our problems? Or do we believe that the next love affair, the new job, those longed-for children, will make our lives go right? Did the crowds of Palm Sunday have that expectation? Did they expect that their welcome to the Messiah would be the end of the story? Were they – are we – hoping for the Hollywood ending?

Maybe they did, and most likely we sometimes do. But we are all going to be disappointed. The Messiah that these crowds were welcoming arriving on his donkey did not make everything easier. On the contrary, they seemed to get harder in what must have been a very shocking way. Jesus did not set about expelling the Romans but marched into the Temple and told the faithful that they were doing everything wrong. He told these people of deep faith that what they thought would lead them to God was defiling a holy place. He turned their expectations of what the Messiah would bring upside down. He called them out of their expectations of what might happen into the harsh reality of examining their own actions, their own priorities, their own way of living out faith. This was devastating and shocking, deeply hurtful and disorienting. And the people reacted by hitting out, by condemning the very Messiah they had begun by celebrating. They could not make the transition to the reality of what he had come to proclaim. They could not see that by beginning with him, going his road, they might have achieved what they wanted, even if in a rather different way.

Joy is important. It is vital that we do not lose our ability to celebrate the wonderful things that happen in our lives. But that joy must be rooted in reality. And our expectations must also be rooted in reality. The challenge of Palm Sunday is not to exclaim over the failure of those crowds to hold to their own proclamation of the coming of Jesus the Messiah. Rather, Palm Sunday, and our knowledge of what comes after, calls us to examine our own expectations, our own habits, our own patterns of living, to look into our hearts, to see where our own expectations are unrealistic, stopping us from growing, to look at where we are comfortable or cosy, at where we have placed our confidence in temples which need to be cleansed. And when we are ready for those temples to be cleansed, when we can live rooted in reality, then we can and will find that we can welcome Christ into our hearts with joyful confidence.

Lord Jesus Christ,
as you rode into Jerusalem,
crowds of people rejoiced and praised,
then turned away and abandoned you.
We pray that we may remain with you,
confessing your name
even in those places where you are scorned.
Amen.[1]

10

Welcomed into the community of love – Maundy Thursday

Before the festival of the Passover, Jesus knew that his hour had come to depart from this world and go to the Father. Having loved his own who were in the world, he loved them to the end. The devil had already put it into the heart of Judas son of Simon Iscariot to betray him. And during supper Jesus, knowing that the Father had given all things into his hands, and that he had come from God and was going to God, got up from the table, took off his outer robe, and tied a towel around himself. Then he poured water into a basin and began to wash the disciples' feet and to wipe them with the towel that was tied around him. He came to Simon Peter, who said to him, 'Lord, are you going to wash my feet?' Jesus answered, 'You do not know now what I am doing, but later you will understand.' Peter said to him, 'You will never wash my feet.' Jesus answered, 'Unless I wash you, you have no share with me.' Simon Peter said to him, 'Lord, not my feet only but also my hands and my head!' Jesus said to him, 'One who has bathed does not need to wash, except for the feet, but is entirely clean. And you are clean, though not all of you.' For he knew who was to betray him; for this reason he said, 'Not all of you are clean.' After he had washed their feet, had put on his robe, and had returned to the table, he said to them, 'Do you know what I have done to you? You call me Teacher and Lord – and you are right, for that is what I am. So if I, your Lord and Teacher, have washed your feet, you also ought

to wash one another's feet. For I have set you
an example, that you also should do as I have
done to you.'

John 13.1-15

A few years ago, my mother visited India. This was
part of a series of exchanges between the Ashbourne
Deanery in the Diocese of Derby and their partner
Diocese of Patma in the Church of North India.

The group travelled widely, and visited a good
number of places: schools and hospitals, churches
and homes. On the whole they were taken in cars or a
minibus, but sometimes they couldn't get through;
the roads were jammed solid or impassable, and then
they had to walk. One evening, after a day when they
had travelled a long distance, a great deal of it on
foot, they arrived at their destination, dusty and tired
and footsore.

At the door their hosts were waiting for them with
bowls of warm steaming water, lightly perfumed, and
clean towels. The hosts invited their guests to sit
down and to take off their shoes. And then the hosts
washed their guests' feet.

My mother said it was the best welcome she had
ever had: at the end of a long journey, dirty and tired,
to be asked to sit down and have her feet washed and
patted dry by her host, to allow herself to be cared
for, to put her tired feet in the hands of another, to be
ministered to.

When she told me the story, I began to see that
there is more to the story of Jesus' washing the feet of
his disciples than simply an act of service. As the one
who washes the disciples' feet, Jesus takes the role of
the servant, as he points out himself. But at the same

time he takes the role of the host who affirms that these guests are worthy of his attention, that all of them – even the one who will betray him, even the extravagantly inept Peter – are worthy of his attention, his tenderness, his care, his welcome. His washing of their feet is an attentive welcome into the community of love, the community of the new commandment, the community of those who love one another as Jesus Christ loves us, who serve one another as Christ serves us.

As we explore the meaning of our faith more deeply, we realise that following Christ and weaving ourselves into the community of love is not a matter of being on one side or another. It is not that we are either servants or served, either ministers or ministered to, either foot washers or those who have their feet washed. All of us are both. All of us serve and all of us are served. This was what Peter had to learn: that his Master and Teacher, whom he revered, could also serve him, Peter. The doctor Sheila Cassidy has written:

> The hardest thing for those of us who are professional carers is to admit that we are in need, to peel off our sweaty socks and let someone else wash our dirty blistered feet. And when at last we have given in and allowed someone to care for us, perhaps there is a certain inertia that makes us want to cling to the role of patient, reluctant to take up the task of caring once more. It is easy to forget that so much caring, so much serving is done by people who are weary and in some way not quite whole.[1]

It is not necessary to be a superstar, to be perfect, in order to serve others. Indeed, those who know and admit that they are not quite whole may have more to offer than those who think that they have nothing to learn. As we open ourselves to that need in us, we may move beyond the clear boundaries of our expectations about who gives and who receives. John Bell tells a story about teachers which challenges our familiar expectations:

> I met him on the train. He said he was in education, learning for life he called it. I said I was interested in education too, so he invited me to come with him to where he taught and learned.
>
> In the corner was an old man with a white stick. Beside him sat a girl reading him a newspaper. 'Nice to see the young helping the blind,' I said. 'Oh,' he replied, 'he's teaching her how to see.'
>
> Across the room came a wheelchair. A paraplegic boy of 18 sat in it. And a boy the same age pushed it. 'It's great when friends help each other,' I said. 'Yes,' he replied, 'the boy in the chair is teaching the other how to walk.'
>
> An old woman lay in bed at the other end of the room. She was covered in open sores. Another woman, much younger, was dressing her wounds. 'Is she a nurse?' I asked. 'Yes,' he replied, 'the old woman is a nurse. She's teaching the other how to care.'
>
> A group doctor was talking to a group of young couples about family planning. He spoke slowly and clearly and used sign language. 'Deaf people need to know about these things as well,' I said. 'Oh, they know,' he said. 'They are teaching the doctor how to listen.'
>
> Confused and not knowing what to say, I sat down. After a while I felt I could speak.

'Seeing all this,' I said, 'I want to pray. I want to thank God that I have my faculties, I now realise that I can do much to help.'

But he said, 'I don't want to upset your devotional life, but I hope that you will also pray to know your own need, and I hope that you will never be afraid to be touched, to be ministered to, to learn from those you thought you were sent to.'[2]

Those of us who are weary and in some way not quite whole – which is to say, all of us – need the comfort and tenderness of having our feet washed, our wounds bound, our needs cared for, as we are welcomed into the kingdom of love. But those of us who are weary and in some way not quite whole – which is to say, all of us – are also those who reach out and care, who wash feet, bind wounds, offer comfort and tenderness, and welcome the world into the love of Christ. It is this vision of mutuality that characterises the community of love into which Jesus invites us. And if we find ourselves sometimes wanting to deny our neediness, our vulnerability, wanting only to give, unable to realise or to express our own neediness, we might remind ourselves of how Christ, too, allowed himself to be ministered to, by a woman who anointed his feet with expensive ointment and wiped it away with her hair, so that the whole house was filled with the fragrance of the perfume (John 12.1-8; and compare Luke 7.36-50).

[Jesus said:] 'I give you a new commandment, that you love one another. Just as I have loved you, you also should love one another. By this everyone will know that you are my disciples, if you have love for one another.'

John 13.34-35

11

Forsaken even by God –
Good Friday

> When they came to the place called The
> Skull, they crucified Jesus there with the
> criminals, one on his right and one on his left.
> Then Jesus said, 'Father, forgive them; for they
> do not know what they are doing.'
>
> Luke 23.33-34

We do not know what we do. We cannot always
know what we do, the consequences of what we do,
for the future is unknown, the consequences of what
we do are hidden.

The disciples did not know that following Jesus
would lead them here, to this cross, this place of
horrible execution. Nor do we know where our
following of Christ will take us.

But sometimes we do know what we do, but refuse
to know. Sometimes what we do is hidden from us, by
our blindness, by our carelessness, by our
insensitivities, by our pressing need to get the job
done and get it done properly.

We cannot always know what we do – but
sometimes we can. Sometimes we need to stop, to
look at our lives, our assumptions, our actions. To ask
ourselves: are my hands holding that hammer? Could
it be me, driving in those nails?

> One of the criminals who were hanged there
> kept deriding him and saying, 'Are you not the
> Messiah? Save yourself and us!' But the other
> rebuked him, saying, 'Do you not fear God,

since you are under the same sentence of condemnation? And we indeed have been condemned justly, for we are getting what we deserve for our deeds, but this man has done nothing wrong.' Then he said, 'Jesus, remember me when you come into your kingdom.' He replied: 'Truly I tell you, today you will be with me in Paradise.'

Luke 23.39-43

Can we acknowledge what we do? Can we be big enough, generous enough, courageous enough to admit to our faults and our failings? Can we swallow our pride, our fear, our wish to preserve appearances and look our Christ in the eye and say, 'That was me'? Can we be brave enough to take the consequences – however unseen – of our own actions, to say, 'Lord, I did it; because of what I did this has come to pass.'

And, having acknowledged our sin, forced ourselves to look at what we have done, can we ask forgiveness; can we, with this man, say: 'Lord, take me with you into your paradise, take me with you on your way, through the pain and the humiliation, the wrongs and the failures; take me with you, take me as I am, with all my imperfections, let me come with you on your road.'

And then, can we accept that forgiveness? Can we accept his invitation? 'Come with me. Today you will be with me in paradise.'

You, as you are. I, as I am.

When Jesus saw his mother and the disciple whom he loved standing beside her, he said to his mother, 'Woman, here is your son.' Then he said to the disciple, 'Here is your mother.' And from that hour the disciple took her into his own home.

John 19.26-27

At this place where there is no love, there is yet love. At this place where the final rejection is played out, there is yet acceptance. At this place where all loyalties are broken down, new relationships are yet forged. At the foot of the cross all are alone, and yet all are together, bound in despair, futility, fear – and yes, by love, and sharing, and acceptance.

> At three o'clock Jesus cried out with a loud voice, 'Eloi, Eloi, lema sabachthani?' which means, 'My God, my God, why have you forsaken me?'
>
> Mark 15.34

There come the times when there seems to be nothing, when no one is there, when there are only the cries of loss and abandonment.

There come the times when we share the cry of Jesus: 'My God, my God, why have you forsaken me?' And in that sharing, in that cry, we know: God has been here too.

> After this ... [Jesus said,] 'I am thirsty.' A jar full of sour wine was standing there. So they put a sponge full of the wine on a branch of hyssop and held it to his mouth.
>
> John 19.28-29

I am thirsty. I need what you have to offer. I need you.

I need you to make yourself vulnerable, to risk standing beside me, to find a way to reach out to me.

I need you to stretch your hand into this place of darkness and pain, to come with me into this place of no return, this place where it is only possible to go on, to go through, to break through the darkness, to taste the living water, to find God.

> When Jesus had received the wine, he said, 'It is finished.'
>
> John 19.30a

> Then Jesus, crying with a loud voice, said, 'Father, into your hands I commend my spirit.' Having said this, he breathed his last.
>
> Luke 23.46

It is finished, but it has only just begun.
His end is our beginning.
To you, Lord, we give ourselves.
To you, Lord, we offer our lives,
    in fullness and in emptiness,
    in grief and in joy,
    in comfort and in pain,
    in darkness and in light.
To you we dedicate what has been,
    what is,
    and what is to come,
confident in the knowledge that you died that we might live.

12

The mystery at the heart of things – Easter Sunday

On the first day of the week, at early dawn, [the women] came to the tomb, taking the spices that they had prepared. They found the stone rolled away from the tomb, but when they went in, they did not find the body. While they were perplexed about this, suddenly two men in dazzling clothes stood beside them. The women were terrified and bowed their faces to the ground, but the men said to them, 'Why do you look for the living among the dead? He is not here, but has risen. Remember how he told you, while he was still in Galilee, that the Son of Man must be handed over to sinners, and be crucified, and on the third day rise again.' Then they remembered his words, and returning from the tomb, they told all this to the eleven and to all the rest. Now it was Mary Magdalene, Joanna, Mary the mother of James, and the other women with them who told this to the apostles. But these words seemed to them an idle tale, and they did not believe them. But Peter got up and ran to the tomb; stooping and looking in, he saw the linen cloths by themselves; then he went home, amazed at what had happened.

Luke 24.1-12

There is a mystery at the heart of things. The mystery at the heart of Luke's story of the resurrection is a strange absence, the mystery of the empty tomb, of the absence of the body of the Lord. There is nothing else. There is no early morning encounter with the risen Lord in Luke's Gospel. There is simply an absence. And angels. Angels, men dressed in dazzling raiment who terrify the women, who tell them that they are looking in the wrong place. 'Why do you look for the living among the dead?'

There is a mystery at the heart of things. In some churches the liturgy of Maundy Thursday includes a Eucharist to mark the celebration of the Last Supper. During the Gloria the organ and the church bells ring out for the last time until Easter Sunday morning. And at the close of the Eucharist the altar is stripped, the candles are carried away, and the reserved sacrament is taken from the tabernacle. In the Old Catholic church in Essen, the tabernacle for the reserved sacrament is integrated into the centre of the altar. On Maundy Thursday evening the door is opened and the sacrament carried away. From then until Easter Sunday morning, the door of the tabernacle stands open, revealing – nothing. An empty space, an absence, at the heart of the altar. The emptiness, the absence speaks deeply. Christ is not where we expect him to be; he is gone: betrayed and on trial, tortured and crucified. He is not where we put him, safe in the box behind the altar, not protected in church, but bleeding and suffering with the many, many people who bleed and suffer in this world; with those whom we cause to suffer, and with us when we suffer ourselves. In those days when the tabernacle is empty, when Christ is absent, it is because he is with us. He is gone. And yet on Easter Sunday morning we celebrate the fact that in that absence he is present amongst us.

On that first Easter morning, Christ was not where the women expected him to be either. He was dead, and his body had been laid in the tomb. Through the long day of the Sabbath the women who had been his friends, who had watched him die in agony, had waited to do for him all that they could still do: anoint his body, preserve it with spices, wrap it in linen cloths and lay it to rest, the suffering come to an end, his agony stilled by death. He had been with them and had lived with them; they had watched with horror as he suffered and died before them and there was nothing more for them to do. Perhaps their only hope was that the ritual, familiar act of preparing the body might bring some consolation. And so they went to the tomb. And he was not there.

Christ is not where the women expected him to be; he is gone. Gone – where? This absence, too, speaks deeply, mysteriously, for in the emptiness come two messengers of God, asking them to look again. 'Why do you look for the living among the dead?' Look for Christ, not in the tomb where you laid him, but with the living: walking with the disciples on the road to Emmaus, welcoming fishermen back to the shore, in the midst of life, physical and there. Look for Christ, not dead, but alive, with the living, hope breaking through despair, light breaking through darkness, joy breaking through grief. Christ is not gone; he is not where they are looking. He is absent. And yet at the same time, somehow, he is present and alive.

This is the deepest mystery, the mystery at the heart of things, the mystery that says that death is not the end. This is the mystery of our faith: that Christ has died and Christ is risen. That in his absence there is a presence. That the empty tomb is not a 'gone away', but a 'come back', proclaiming the advent of the risen Christ into our lives. It is the mystery of this advent, of the continuing and disturbing presence of Christ, that is the central mystery of Easter, the continuing unsettling reality of the resurrection. Christ is gone, yet Christ is here. Christ is absent, and yet present. Christ is crucified and dead, but Christ is risen and alive.

The women at the tomb felt the absence and in it were called to believe. Here the women do not encounter the risen Christ at the tomb, in the garden; for Luke that is left to the two disciples making their weary way back to Emmaus. The women encounter only the emptiness of the tomb, and the reminder of Christ's promise. And they believe: they believe what they have heard; they believe that this absence means more than an end, an emptiness, a predictable end to an unpredictable story. And they turn, and they run, and they tell the story in their turn.

The women's news of absence and promise is not what the other disciples expect to hear. Safe in the certainty that women cannot be trusted as witnesses, they do not believe. Or do they? Peter goes running, perhaps to prove them wrong, perhaps to see for himself. And he sees – what? Nothing but an absence, and in it the winding cloths. No angels. Just the empty tomb. And he is amazed.

We want to see for ourselves too. The great temptation at Easter is not to believe, to ask for proof, to seek explanations; to want to make everything safe and predictable; to bind God's actions to the way the world works; to put everything neatly in its place, labelled and explained; to lock the risen Christ up in a box, a tabernacle, a cave, a theory.

We can try. But Christ will not stay there. The risen Christ breaks out of our categories, breaks down our safe distinctions, rolls away the stones from our minds and reveals our rituals to be empty. Christ breaks out and through, and is gone, leaving us with nothing – and yet with so much: with the demand that we look elsewhere, with the call that we start again, with the promise of the encounter with the living God.

This is the miracle of Easter. Rowan Williams suggests that 'the one thing we can say with confidence' about the first Easter is that it heralded 'the advent of the Church – of a new style of corporate human life – and of its proclamation of release from the prison of mutual destructiveness'.[1] The important question for us must then surely be, 'What will happen to us this Easter to release us and others from destructiveness?' How will the absence that is the presence of Christ lead us to live anew, sharing with each other the living love of God that overcomes death? Where do we encounter the healing, reconciling love of God? How do we believe and live out our faith? Where do the empty spaces in our lives tell us to look? Where are our new beginnings?

As we seek the answers to these questions – that is, as we live out our response to Easter – all of us will be tempted to seek the risen Christ only in the places we expect him, in the familiar places we have designed for him, in the tabernacles and rituals by which we order our faith and our lives. We all seek the risen Christ where we are sure he is to be found, and again and again we will find that he is not there. Instead the door is open, the stone rolled back, and there is an absence. And in that absence the conviction of the unexpected presence of the risen Christ.

O unfamiliar God,
we seek you in the places you have already left,
and fail to see you
even when you stand before us.
Grant us so to recognise your strangeness
that we need not cling to our familiar grief,
but may be freed to proclaim resurrection
in the name of Christ. Amen.[2]

Christ is risen! Alleluia!

13

Encountering Christ in the garden – the first week of Easter

Mary stood weeping outside the tomb. As she wept, she bent over to look into the tomb, and she saw two angels in white, sitting where the body of Jesus had been lying, one at the head and the other at the feet. They said to her, 'Woman, why are you weeping?' She said to them, 'They have taken away my Lord, and I do not know where they have laid him.' When she had said this, she turned round and saw Jesus standing there, but she did not know that it was Jesus. Jesus said to her, 'Woman, why are you weeping? For whom are you looking?' Supposing him to be the gardener, she said to him, 'Sir, if you have carried him away, tell me where you have laid him, and I will take him away.' Jesus said to her, 'Mary!' She turned and said to him in Hebrew, 'Rabbouni!' (which means Teacher). Jesus said to her, 'Do not hold on to me, because I have not yet ascended to the Father. But go to my brothers and say to them "I am ascending to my Father and your Father, to my God and your God." ' Mary Magdalene went and announced to the disciples, 'I have seen the Lord'; and she told them that he had said these things to her.

John 20.11-18

All that we know about how the world works tells us that none of this could have happened. People just don't rise from the dead and meet us the garden. Our reason tells us that when people are dead they stay dead; so that what happened to Mary Magdalene in the garden is simply not how things are. Looked at with the light of reason, the events of Easter are really not very likely.

And yet, we celebrate Easter, the risen Christ. It may not be likely, but because we are marking this event, this encounter, it seems that the highly improbable is yet entirely possible. The Lord is risen; he is risen indeed. Alleluia! The Lord is risen; the crucifixion is not the end of the story; nor does the story end with Mary's encounter with the risen Christ in the garden. Today, in this Easter celebration, we are reminded that this encounter is for all of us. It is for all of us to proclaim, 'This is the Lord for whom we have waited; let us be glad and rejoice in his salvation.'

Easter is about proclamation, about passing on the good news, about faith – our faith now. At Easter the risen Christ brings us a new order which we live and experience, which changes the way we experience and see the world. Stephen Sykes has written, 'It seems that the manifestation of the resurrection requires the obscure reality of at least one changed life. Mine.'[1] Easter is about encounter and change – about how Mary's encounter with Christ in the garden can become our own life-changing encounter with Christ. It is about meeting a stranger and recognising in them the face of Christ. It is about grasping what is possible.

It is easy to get distracted from this by concerns about what actually happened. But, in fact, the message of Easter has very little to do with trying to find out what really happened or with trying to read some kind of empirical truth into the narrative of the Easter story. On one level, the events recounted in the Easter story may not be likely, but does that mean that none of it is true, none of it is possible? Mary's story is the story of an encounter with Christ, a confession of faith, and when we talk about faith we must constantly remind ourselves that things are not always as simple as our reason would sometimes have us believe.

The essential aspect of Mary's encounter in the garden is that she does not stop to think 'This can't be true.' She doesn't stop to worry that there is no way that this can be Christ; she simply recognises him and is joyful.

The philosopher Isabelle Stengers suggests that to say that something is possible is to describe a new way of seeing things:

> When it is a question of probabilities the requirement is that the situation be well-defined.... When it is a question of what may happen, of possibility and becoming, what is pivotal is the commitment of those who discern it, the way in which their action or way of life attests to it and makes it real for others. ... The possible only exists through its witnesses.[2]

The witness of faith allows what is possible to override what is probable, to see that what is probable or predictable is not at all the same as what is possible. There are occasions when what we expect, what seems likely, simply is not what occurs. We can probably all think of times in our lives when our expectations have been entirely misleading, when things turned out much better – or much worse – than we had any right to expect. Times when improbability, and not probability, seemed to be the ruling factor in determining what was possible. Times when joy broke through, even in moments of the most shattering despair.

> Prayer is a silence and a shouting
> a burst of praise
> a thanksgiving
> welling up and out of us
> in spite of everything

wrote Kathy Keay after being diagnosed with breast cancer in 1993.[3] Faith wells up and out of us, in praise and thanksgiving, in spite of everything. Faith has everything to do with what is possible.

It seems to me that Mary's encounter with the risen Christ is an encounter in which what is probable has been entirely subverted by what is possible. Mary's faith allows her to see and to recognise in what she had not expected – what she knew could not be – the living Christ. Faith allows Mary to look and to see, and then to bear witness. Her faith enables what is possible to take over from what was probable.

Part of celebrating Easter is a reaffirmation that reason is not all of what faith is about. Our reason tends to lead us to expect the world to be an orderly place in which patterns which have worked in the past will also work in the future. In science and in daily life we use our reason to predict what will happen – that the sun will 'rise' at a certain time tomorrow; that my car will start; that it will take such and such a time to get to wherever I am trying to go. When we do that we are extrapolating from our experience of the past into the future. In sense we are predicting the future according to what is probable. All that is fine so long as we do not become in our expectations, expecting our experience of the past, and our interpretation of that experience, to determine all that can be known about the future.

For faith, reason, probability and expectation are not everything. For Kathy Keay, the extraordinary discovery is that prayer is praise and thanksgiving that wells up and out of us, in spite of everything: in spite of a diagnosis that proved to be a death sentence. For Mary the astonishing truth was that she met Christ in the garden: in spite of a death that should have proved final. The deep truth is in the encounter, rather than in arguments about whether or not this encounter could scientifically have taken place. What is important is that we enter into it, not by suspending judgement, but by acknowledging that our judgement, our reason, does not comprehend everything.

In a very different way, and a very different mood, T.S. Eliot reminds us of this too:

If you came this way,
Taking any route, starting from anywhere,
At any time or at any season,
It would always be the same:
    you would have to put off
Sense and notion. You are not here to verify,
Instruct yourself, or inform curiosity
Or carry report. You are here to kneel
Where prayer has been valid.
    And prayer is more
Than an order of words,
    the conscious occupation
Of the praying mind, or the sound
    of the voice praying.[4]

If you are to go this way, you have to put off sense and notion, to remember that prayer – and with it faith – is not about factual report, about instruction and information, about verification or falsification. Of course faith is rooted in our world; of course our encounters with God, our meeting with the risen

Christ take place in contexts and in places and with people we know. But in faith we may find that we know them and yet do not know them at the same time. In faith we may recognise and at the same time be utterly surprised; we may find the unfamiliar breaking through the familiar, the possible tearing apart the probable.

Mary in the garden encountered a gardener who was not a gardener at all, but the beloved teacher whom she mourned. And she listened to what he had to say and carried the news to her fellow disciples. In her mourning, in all the pain of death and sadness, she was able nonetheless not to cling to what had been before, but to grasp something entirely new, to break free of what was simply probable, predictable. Can we break free too? Are we open to encountering the possible, to recognising that which God makes possible? Are we open to the encounter with God, with the risen Christ, which changes our lives so that we, too, may carry the message to others? I hope so. For the joy of Easter is also about us, about 'the obscure reality of at least one changed life'. It is about the ways in which the encounter with the risen Christ changes each of us – you, and me.

> Living God,
> as we celebrate the resurrection of your Son,
> you fill us with new life
> and lasting joy.
> Be always close to us in your Son,
>   who is our Brother,
> open our eyes to recognise him in our lives,
> and direct our lives
>   always according to his ways,
> that we may be led by him to you,
> and through the Holy Spirit
> praise and glorify you for ever. Amen.[5]

14

Turning to Christ in doubt – the second week of Easter

When it was evening on that day, the first day of the week, and the doors of the house where the disciples had met were locked for fear of the Jews, Jesus came and stood among them and said, 'Peace be with you.' After he said this, he showed them his hands and his side. Then the disciples rejoiced when they saw the Lord. Jesus said to them again, 'Peace be with you. As the Father has sent me, so I send you.' When he had said this, he breathed on them and said to them, 'Receive the Holy Spirit. If you forgive the sins of any, they are forgiven them; if you retain the sins of any, they are retained.'

But Thomas (who was called the Twin), one of the twelve, was not with them when Jesus came. So the other disciples told him, 'We have seen the Lord.' But he said to them, 'Unless I see the mark of the nails in his hands, and put my finger in the mark of the nails and my hand in his side, I will not believe.' A week later, his disciples were again in the house, and Thomas was with them. Although the doors were shut, Jesus came and stood among them and said, 'Peace be with you.' Then he said to Thomas, 'Put your finger here and see my hands. Reach out your hand and put it in my side. Do not doubt but believe.' Thomas answered him, 'My Lord and my God!' Jesus said to him, 'Have you believed because you have seen me? Blessed are those who have not seen and yet have come to believe.'

John 20.19-29

Doubting Thomas we call him, with perhaps a certain amount of complacency, as if we know we wouldn't have been like him. But is this fair? How would you have felt? Imagine it was your best friend, your teacher, executed last week, before your eyes. How would you feel? Despair? Horror? Guilt at not having been able to stop it? Disbelief that this could ever have happened at all? A pain that you couldn't believe would ever go away? Perhaps resentment that you had allowed yourself to be led into this, or terror that it could happen to you next?

And then, in the midst of your grief, your friends, your colleagues tell you he's been with them. These are people you thought you knew and could trust. You've been through a lot together, had some good laughs, faced the difficult times, shared food when there was not much to share, learned some hard, unexpected lessons. And now this. You didn't bargain for their coming up with such a sick joke, you thought they felt as awful about all this as you do, you thought they were in despair too. No wonder Thomas was angry, no wonder he came up with such a sharp rejoinder. 'I don't believe it. I don't believe it, and I won't believe it until I see him myself and put my hands there where the nails were, touch the wound in his side.'

Doubting Thomas? Perhaps, rather, it was despairing Thomas. For it must have been a deeply painful moment for him. In the midst of his grief for Jesus, his friend and his teacher, he must have felt even more utterly betrayed and abandoned by what would have seemed the cruel behaviour of the rest of his friends. Thomas was in despair.

Except that it wasn't a sick joke. The circle of disciples, sheltering behind closed doors in fear of what had happened to Jesus, really had seen ... well, what? Who? To them had been vouchsafed an encounter that left them knowing that they had seen the Lord, that Christ was with them, that they had not been left alone in their grief. An encounter which showed them Christ risen; Christ with them, Christ wishing them peace, giving them the strength, the Spirit to go on. And it was this that they were trying to offer him, this comfort, this hope, that Thomas couldn't at first see or accept, because he knew it could not be.

And then Thomas saw too. In the midst of his despair, his anger, his grief, Christ came to him, invited him to touch the wounds in his risen body. And the closed eyes of Thomas' angry, black despair were opened and he recognised Christ. He could say, 'Yes, Lord, it is you. I see you, you are with me.'

Those wounds that the disciples had seen, that Thomas wanted to touch in order to be convinced, are not just identification, not simply some kind of reassurance that this really is Jesus, the risen Christ. Rather they are reminders of Jesus' own dreadful suffering, his aloneness on the cross. They are the demonstration that the risen Christ is that same Jesus who had suffered so terribly, who had been alone in that dark place of pain and terror and grief. Jesus' wounds are a reminder of all that has happened, and they reassure Thomas that he had good reasons for his grief.

So Thomas sees, and believes. He experiences the miracle of the risen Christ, the stunning shock of the resurrection. And then? It cannot have been a simple matter of rushing off to celebrate. The experience of the risen Christ was – and is – not a facile removal of grief, a smoothing out of trouble. Thomas cannot simply say, 'So Christ is risen; everything is all right after all.' Christ's presence after the resurrection is surely different from Jesus' company during his life, even if only because the people to whom he appeared have been changed through his death. For the resurrection does not and cannot cancel out the crucifixion. The resurrection puts the crucifixion in a new perspective, gives it an entirely new dimension, but the grief and the pain and the anger cannot simply vanish. And yet something essential changes for Thomas and the other disciples. The world looks different. They have not lost all hope; their friend, their teacher, is with them after all, offering them a chance to build a new and different relationship, offering them in the midst of grief, terror and death the deep hope of new life. There is a way forward through the pain; there is the possibility of growth, of change, of creation. There is a light in the darkness that wasn't there before.

Thomas' experience reminds us that faith is not a panacea, not a remedy for all problems. The encounter with Christ offers no easy answers; in fact, it may not offer any answers at all. But Thomas' encounter with the risen Christ offers hope to set against the pain and grief and despair that he feels. It does not take them away, and it does not seem to offer Thomas any explanation. Christ does not invite Thomas to embark on an intellectual discussion of the problem of evil. Rather, his is an immediate experience, which fulfils his need to touch and be touched, allows him to hear and respond to Christ. It is an encounter which offers him comfort and strength, but it does so in a way which may have left him with more questions than he started with.

So it is also for us. Belief in God, encounter with Christ, our own experience of the shock of resurrection: none of these offers a neat answer to all our questions and difficulties. Rather, the encounter with God offers new possibilities, new ways forward – and with them new challenges. It brings comfort, the promise we are not alone, but it may not bring ease. It offers the reassurance that even in our darkest moments of grief, even when we feel most deeply betrayed, even in our most terrible moments of fear, even when we feel that we have failed miserably, even then Christ is there, giving us strength, encouraging us to find a new beginning. Thomas' encounter with God, his recognition of Christ even in the midst of his stubborn, despairing rejection of the hope he had been offered, offers us, too, the hope that God can and does and will work in us, be recognised by us, despite our blindness, our closed-ness, our inadequacy. The disciples had failed Jesus in the last hours before his death, but they were not precluded from witnessing his resurrection. Instead, they were the first. Perhaps it may be in those moments when we feel most inadequate and shut off, that we are most sure that we cannot believe, that we are in truth most open to experiencing the contradiction of our human values and expectations and encountering the risen Christ.

This is not to suggest that we experience God only when we are in the depths of despair. But it is in those moments that we are more vulnerable and less sure of what the answers should be. Maybe the hope is easier to grasp at such times. Maybe it is easier when we are in the middle of such a dark time to believe without being sure, without looking for proof; to appreciate the importance of a glimmer of light. Maybe at such times we are in greater need of God's presence and therefore more open to seeing it. Maybe at such times we are more ready to accept that we do not have to see everything, that we do not even necessarily have to understand what we are doing. What God asks of us is not to seek answers, but to recognise him and respond; to see him, and seeing him to cry out: 'My Lord and my God!' In our confession of Christ, God can use us, as we are in ourselves, in our frailty and distress – if we are open to him.

Being open to being used, to allowing our lives to reflect the contradictions and the struggles, and the joys and love too, to not having all the answers – it is this that is the leap of faith.

> 'Blessed are those who have not seen
>   and yet believe.'
> Blessed are those who cannot see,
>   and whose eyes are yet opened.
> Blessed are those who are blinded by fear,
>   and who are yet given the courage to believe.
> 'Blessed are those who have not seen
>   and yet believe.'

15

Recognising Christ at the table – the third week of Easter

On that same day two of them were going to a village called Emmaus, about seven miles from Jerusalem, and talking with each other about all these things that had happened. While they were talking and discussing, Jesus himself came near and went with them, but their eyes were kept from recognizing him. And he said to them, 'What are you discussing with each other while you walk along?' They stood still, looking sad. Then one of them, whose name was Cleopas, answered him, 'Are you the only stranger in Jerusalem who does not know the things that have taken place there in these days?' He asked them, 'What things?' They replied, 'The things about Jesus of Nazareth, who was a prophet mighty in deed and word before God and all the people, and how our chief priests and leaders handed him over to be condemned to death and crucified him. But we had hoped that he was the one to redeem Israel. Yes, and besides all this, it is now the third day since these things took place. Moreover, some women of our group astounded us. They were at the tomb early this morning, and when they did not find his body there, they came back and told us that they had indeed seen a vision of angels who said that he was alive. Some of those who were with us went to the tomb and found it just as the women had said; but they did not see him.' Then he said, 'Oh, how foolish you are, and how slow of heart to believe all that the prophets have declared! Was it not necessary that the Messiah should suffer these things and then enter into his glory?' Then beginning with Moses and all the prophets, he interpreted to them the things about himself in all the scriptures.

As they came near the village to which they were going, he walked ahead as if he were going on. But they urged him strongly, saying, 'Stay with us, because it is almost evening, and the day is now nearly over.' So he went in to stay with them. When he was at the table with them, he took bread, blessed and broke it, and gave it to them. Then their eyes were opened, and they recognized him; and he vanished from their sight. They said to each other, 'Were our hearts not burning within us while he was talking to us on the road, while he was opening the scriptures to us?' That same hour they got up and returned to Jerusalem; and they found the eleven and their companions gathered together. They were saying, 'The Lord has risen indeed, and he has appeared to Simon.' Then they told what had happened on the road, and how he had been made known to them in the breaking of the bread.

Luke 24.13-35

The Bible abounds with meals and invitations to meals. Probably we think first of the Last Supper, the Passover meal which Jesus shares with his disciples (Luke 22.14-23). But we might think, too, of Isaiah's prophecy of a banquet for all the peoples and nations, 'a feast of rich food, a feast of well-matured wines' (Isaiah 25.6-9). Or the table to which Wisdom calls the simple: 'Come, eat of my bread and drink of the wine I have mixed' (Proverbs 9.1-6). Or of Revelation's marriage supper for the Lamb: 'Blessed are those who are invited' (Revelation 19.6-9). And here we have Luke's account of a simple breaking of bread by hungry travellers at the end of a tiring walk (Luke 24.13-35).

Many meals: some festive, some simple. In our lives, we too spend time eating: at table, or perhaps in front of the television; alone, or with others; in joyful elaborate celebration and in ordinary daily life. As Christian communities, we also meet to share a meal: to celebrate the Eucharist, Holy Communion, the Mass. We meet together to share bread and wine, and later, perhaps, we will eat and drink together in a rather more ordinary way, with coffee and biscuits. And later again, with family or friends, over the supper or dinner table, at breakfast. So it goes on. It is a very ordinary thing, this sharing of food, this gathering at table.

A meal may be an ordinary thing, but this simple sharing of food and fellowship is central to all those invitations to meals, whether heavenly or otherwise, and central to the encounter with the risen Christ at Emmaus. This meeting for a meal, the offer of hospitality to the stranger met on the road, the breaking of bread together is a very ordinary thing, a simple action, an everyday occurrence – but it is here that the disciples recognise the stranger, here that the disciples see that their companion is Jesus. Surely, we might think, they should have recognised him sooner, they should have heard his voice in his theological explications of the scriptures, his interpretation of the passages that prophesied his coming, in his wisdom and his learning?

But it is not in his deep learning that the disciples recognise Jesus, but in his presence at the table, in his breaking and sharing of the bread. It is in the community, in the simple action of sharing, of eating together. It is in the action of sitting around a table, of being together, equal, of fulfilling each other's most basic needs – in this small act of living community – that they realise who he is.

Of course, in recognising Christ the disciples come to understand what he has been telling them. It is then that they take the road back to Jerusalem to share their experience with the other disciples. But it is, I think, significant that the understanding, the urge to share what has happened come after the shared meal, after the realisation that this person with whom they have been travelling, who has stopped to spend time with them, and with whom they are sharing bread, is Jesus, the risen Christ.

For the disciples in Emmaus, the breaking of bread is at first sight a trivial act, but it turns out to be not trivial at all. This act of sitting together around the table to break bread is important, not because through it physical hunger is satisfied – although that is surely an important aspect too – but because it is here that the disciples can look beyond the superficial level of what they have first seen and recognise the presence of God. The meal which they share points beyond itself; it has a meaning which is far beyond the simple action of breaking bread. This meal, this encounter, causes the disciples to look at the world in a different way. The shared meal points beyond itself. It is become sacrament.

Leonardo Boff has written of *Sacraments of Life; Life of the Sacraments*. He describes the way in which simple actions, everyday objects, can become 'signs and symbols of encounter, effort, conquest, and the inner life of the human being. ... The human world, even if it be material and technical, is never merely material and technical. It is symbolic and fraught with meaning.'[1] Our Eucharist is one of those; it is, or should be, a symbol of our community in the risen Christ. Too often it has become a symbol rather of division, between different understandings and interpretations. The disagreements about this sacrament through Church history have been many and deep. In the midst of our divisions it may help to reflect that each of the different terms used to describe this mystery – the Lord's Supper – Holy Communion – Eucharist – Mass — reminds us of a different and important aspect of its meaning and of its calling to us. To speak of the Lord's Supper is to remember the Last Supper (as we do every time we celebrate together) and to mark the truth that our remembering of it together is Christ's gift and instruction to us, to his body, the Church. To speak of Holy Communion is to focus on how we are invited into community and unity with Christ and with each other, to become Christ's body in the world. To speak of Eucharist – thanksgiving – is to express our gratitude and joy at God's continuing gift of God's self to us in creation and salvation. To speak of the Mass, from the Latin *mitto*, to send, is to honour our call to mission, as God sends us out, fed and sustained by Christ, to transform his world.

The important thing is that the Eucharist should be – and at its best is – a place in which we ourselves meet and recognise the risen Christ and are sent out to proclaim him. It may sometimes be that our Eucharist, our church community, our discussions and our thinking and praying together, are more like the discussions of the disciples with Jesus on the road to Emmaus. They may be waiting to be filled with the meaning of the actual encounter with God, the direct encounter with Christ. And if that is so – and why should it not be? – it could be that it is in the simple everyday encounters of daily life that we begin to grasp what all this is really about. Roy Campbell writes of a sailor returning exhausted from a night at sea, for whom the welcome of children bringing food and drink became – on this morning at least – a Mass, a Eucharist:

> But when with food and drink,
>   at morning-light,
> The children met me at the water-side,
> Never was wine so red or bread so white.[2]

A simple gift of food and drink, and the world is more deeply textured and more richly coloured. As Boff says, 'A sacrament does not tear human beings away from this world. It ... [asks] them to look more closely and deeply into the very heart of the world.'[3] It is not in learned words and elevated talk that we learn to know God; but there, at the heart of the world, in the trivialities of daily life, which are not trivial at all, there we meet God, there we may recognise the risen Christ.

> O God, you giver of all life,
> in the breaking of the bread,
> we recognise the risen Christ.
> Feed us with your Word,
> and send us out into the world
> to proclaim your love and your goodness
> and there encounter the risen Christ anew.
> Amen.[4]

16

A passionate love for God –
the fourth week of Easter

When they had finished breakfast, Jesus said to Simon Peter, 'Simon son of John, do you love me more than these?' He said to him, 'Yes, Lord; you know that I love you.' Jesus said to him, 'Feed my lambs.' A second time he said to him, 'Simon son of John, do you love me?' He said to him, 'Yes, Lord; you know that I love you.' Jesus said to him, 'Tend my sheep.' He said to him the third time, 'Simon son of John, do you love me?' Peter felt hurt because he said to him the third time, 'Do you love me?' And he said to him, 'Lord, you know everything; you know that I love you.' Jesus said to him, 'Feed my sheep.'

John 21.15-17

How do I love thee? Let me count the ways.
I love thee to the depth and breadth and height
My soul can reach, when feeling out of sight
For the end of Being and ideal Grace.
I love thee to the level of everyday's
Most quiet need, by sun and candlelight.
I love thee freely, as men strive for Right;
I love thee purely, as they turn from Praise.
I love thee with the passion put to use
In my old griefs, and with my childhood's faith.
I love thee with a love I seemed to lose
With my lost saints – I love thee with the breath,
Smiles, tears of all my life! – and, if God choose,
I shall but love thee better after death.[1]

Elizabeth Barrett Browning wrote her *Sonnets from the Portuguese* for her beloved husband, Robert Browning. It is probably not given to all of us to love as she seems to have done. But as Christians we are, as both the Gospel and the First Epistle of John remind us, called to love. 'I give you a new commandment, that you love one another' (John 13.34). 'Beloved, let us love one another, because love is from God; everyone who loves is born of God and knows God. … Beloved, since God loved us so much, we also ought to love one another' (1 John 4.7; 11). The call to love – to love God, to love neighbour, to love self – is the central call of our faith, as we are reminded in the summary of the Law:

> Our Lord Jesus Christ said: the first commandment is this: 'Hear, O Israel, the Lord our God is the only Lord. You shall love the Lord your God with all your heart, with all your soul, with all your mind, and with all your strength.' The second is this: 'Love your neighbour as yourself.' There is no other commandment greater than these. On these two commandments hang all the law and the prophets.[2]

We are called to love – God, neighbour, self. And to love God above all, with all that we have and all that we are, for the love of others and self will flow from that.

In the face of this great call to love, when we read Elizabeth Barrett Browning's words and the ways in which she experienced love, we may reflect that if we could feel this way about God, it would be not at all a bad statement of faith:

> I love thee to the depth and breadth and height / My soul can reach, / I love thee … by sun and

candlelight. / I love thee freely; / I love thee purely. / I love thee with the passion put to use / In my old griefs, and with my childhood's faith.

If we could say this about our passion for God, then we would be saying a lot, for we would be saying something along these lines: 'I love God as far as my soul can reach. I love God in the bright light of confident faith and in the times when the light of calling seems dim. I love God freely, purely; I love God with the passion and energy I used to spend on other things, with the simplicity and directness and confidence of my faith in childhood.' And if we can say this about our love for God, then surely we have come quite a long way towards fulfilling that first and great commandment.

But can we say it?

'Peter, do you love me?' Jesus asks Peter. 'Yes, Lord,' replies Peter, patiently or not so patiently, perhaps growing less certain as he speaks. Perhaps there are not many of us who can answer this question with an unreserved 'Yes!' Certainly I do not always feel like an ardent soul, longing for, passionate for God. 'Why do you want God?' a group of us were once asked at a meeting for women clergy and ordinands. 'I'm not sure I always do want God,' I had to reply, shamefacedly. 'But God has made one thing abundantly clear: God wants me.' Even when it is difficult to feel that I am not a failure at loving God, it can be a starting point to realise that God wants me, even when I am not sure, or half-hearted. 'God believes in you, even if you don't believe in him,' as Clare is reminded by her father in Sara Maitland's novel *Home Truths*.[3] And just as God does not stop believing in me, so, too, God does not stop loving me, even when I have stopped loving God.

It is out of God's love for me that my love for God springs, a pale reflection of the divine love that encompasses me. And so, if it is possible to read Elizabeth Barrett Browning's sonnet as an expression our love for God, then we may surely read it also as a vision of God's love for us. For God loves each of us as far as our souls can reach – and then some. God loves us in the bright days of our confident faith and in the times when the light of calling seems dim. God loves us freely, purely; with passion and energy, with simplicity and directness and confidence. As John writes: 'Beloved, since God loved us so much, we also ought to love one another.' It is out of God's love for us that we love God, and one another, and ourselves.

It is a strange thing to be called – indeed, not just called, but commanded – to love 'with all your heart, with all your soul, with all your mind, and with all your strength'. We may feel – our experience may be – that love like this is not something that happens on demand, not something that we can turn on like a tap. We may ask ourselves, 'However can we be called to overwhelming love?'

I ask myself too, and must confess that, in the end, I don't know. But that is our calling. And in recognising and seeking to respond to that calling, I wonder whether we sometimes fail because we mistake what love is. Is great love perhaps quieter than we sometimes realise, not the rushing wind or the earthquake, but the still small voice? Can we sometimes be caught up into the outpouring of God's love without really even noticing that this is where we are? Jesus responds to Peter's confession of love by giving him a task, a responsibility: 'Feed my lambs;

tend my sheep.' Let that love show itself in the form of love for others.

A German poet, Walter Hermann Fritz, wrote a very different sort of love poem:

Because you make the days
into ships
which know their direction

Because your body
can laugh.

Because your silence
has texture and depth.

Because a year
takes on the form of your face.

Because through you I understand
what presence is,

I love you.[4]

Perhaps this is the true result of the discovery of the love of God: that our days are made into ships which have direction, that our lives take on meaning, that we begin to understand what presence is, what it is to stand beside someone in their pain, to be accompanied in our grief, that we are able to enter the textured depths of silence, open to joy and beauty, alerted to the tragedy and the jokes of creation. The love of God, being loved by God, loving God, is what gives our lives their shape and form, their texture and their fullness.

And if we feel that we do not know how we love God, or if we do not feel God's love for us, then this may help us too. For perhaps we expect God's love to be more exciting, more challenging, more active than our experience necessarily will be. Perhaps it is in discovering whatever it is that can give our lives shape and meaning, and accepting and participating in that with joy, in love, with passion, with depth, with simplicity, with honesty. Perhaps it is then that we find ourselves truly loving God; when we find what it is for us to feed God's lambs, and tend God's sheep. For in doing the deeds of love, we may bring to others the fruits of the love of God, offering that love to them, even when we feel unable to love ourselves.

How do we love God? Let us count the ways! (Or some of them.) We love God, surely, by offering the assurance of God's love to others. That may mean by taking it into our personal relationships or talking about our faith. But it does not mean that for everyone.

We love God, too, when we are present in the places in the world where there is poverty, when we try to feed the hungry, give shelter to the homeless, minister to the sick. And so we love God when we work with the homeless, when we provide food for those who would otherwise have none.

We love God by praying for others, by holding them up to God in love. We love God by seeking to preserve the world which has been gifted to us in creation.

We love God when we engage ourselves for justice, when we seek to speak out against discrimination.

We love God when we are patient and honest with ourselves, our failings and our strengths, when we have the grace to affirm the presence of Christ in others, their strengths and their failings.

We love God when we can use the gifts we have been granted in the service and in the affirmation of others.

We love God when we spend time waiting and listening to what God wants of us.

In all of this we love God, and the fruits of our love should be that others are offered the experience of God's love as well. This, surely, is the fruit of the vine that is Christ, the fruits by which those who love are known.

> Beloved, let us love one another, because love is from God; everyone who loves is born of God and knows God.
>
> 1 John 4.7

> Beloved, since God loves us so much, we ought also to love one another.
>
> 1 John 4.11

The peace of God –
the fifth week of Easter

Jesus himself stood among them and said to them, 'Peace be with you.' They were startled and terrified, and thought that they were seeing a ghost. He said to them, 'Why are you frightened, and why do doubts arise in your hearts? Look at my hands and my feet; see that it is I myself. Touch me and see; for a ghost does not have flesh and bones as you see that I have.' And when he had said this, he showed them his hands and his feet. While in their joy they were disbelieving and still wondering, he said to them, 'Have you anything here to eat?' They gave him a piece of broiled fish, and he took it and ate it in their presence.

Luke 24.36-43

'Jesus himself stood amongst them and said to them, "Peace be with you."'

These words of peace, which are exchanged in every Anglican Eucharist, are often cited in the resurrection stories. The encounter with the risen Christ is somehow an encounter with peace. The words leave us facing a vital question: what is peace? What is this peace which we find in the presence of the risen Christ? What is the peace of God, which passes all understanding?

This is a question with which many people in the world are confronted daily. It is a question that must tear at the hearts of all who live in places where there is trouble: in Iraq, or Afghanistan, in Israel and Palestine, or the Democratic Republic of Congo. And it is a question that perhaps should especially concern those of us who live in the privilege of the West: we live generally free from war, in some comfort, with considerable security. But we may well ask ourselves whether we really live in peace. Do we live in the kind of peace which leads us to – indeed, which is – the encounter with the risen Christ? Or is this a complacent peace, the kind of false peace about which Ezekiel and Jeremiah warn, which is fêted by the false prophets who cry, 'Peace, peace' where there is no peace? Is our peace founded on God's justice and righteousness, or is it rather a false peace, an island of superficial peace produced and protected by a lack of peace elsewhere, created by the practice of injustice and the perpetration of violence in other places, the result of pretending that everything is all right, of simply ignoring conflict around us?

These are difficult questions, which may fill us with unease, or guilt, or frustration that there is so much wrong in the world and so very little that we apparently can do about it. It is so much easier to turn our back on such uncomfortable questions and to get on with our sheltered lives. It is easier – but will it lead us into the peace of Christ? I think not. For it seems to me that confronting these difficult, unanswerable questions, the pain and the hurt that such questions bring with them, is an essential part of the encounter with the risen Christ. Our recognition that such questions are difficult and painful, our realisation that our world is broken and hurt, our admission that we ourselves collude and fail in so many ways, opens us to meet Christ when he comes to us.

And as we hear the voice of the risen Christ saying, 'Peace be with you!' we may hear also the echo of his earlier words: 'Do you think that I have come to bring peace to the earth?' asks Jesus. 'No, I tell you, but rather division! From now on, five in one household will be divided, three against two and two against three' (Luke 12.51-52). For if we are to be true to Christ's call to peace, the paradox is that division is necessary. The call to peace cannot be heard separately from the call to proclaim God's love and God's justice. Albert Nolan, the South African theologian, writes: 'The peace that God wants is a peace that is based on truth, justice and love. The peace that the world offers us is a superficial peace and unity that compromises the truth, that covers over the injustice, and that is usually settled on for thoroughly selfish purposes.' Following Jesus is 'a matter of promoting truth and justice at all costs, even at the cost of creating conflict and dissention along the way.'[1] Martin Luther King also came to realise that authentic harmony and reconciliation cannot exist without justice:

> A religion that professes a concern for the souls of men and is not equally concerned about the slums that damn them, the economic conditions that strangle them, and the social conditions that cripple them, is a spiritually moribund religion.[2]

Christ's call to peace is a call to wage peace rather than war, to live out love. The paradox is that a central part of the mission of peace may be the creation of conflict, or (more accurately) the uncovering of conflict, of injustice, the exposing and naming of something which is there but not spoken about. To avoid doing this, to act as though injustice does not exist, is not to create the peace to which Christ calls us, but a false peace of avoidance and pretence. For it is not peace, but avoidance, to act as though dissension is not present. It is not peace, but avoidance, to proclaim unity and harmony when there is none.

This can be difficult to accept, for our dream of living out God's love is of harmony and togetherness and not of conflict and dissension. But the truth is, as Dorothy Day has written, that the reality of love lived out is not easy: 'love in action is a harsh and dreadful thing compared to love in dreams'.[3] The reality of the peace of God – which passes all understanding – is that in pursuit of it we are likely to find ourselves wielding the sword of justice and truth. It is a painful, harsh and dreadful reality that brings us to the true peace of the risen Christ.

Should we be surprised at that? When the risen Christ came to the disciples who had abandoned him and said, 'Peace be with you!' he showed them the marks of his wounds, his hands and his side. They saw in his body the pain he had suffered, the pain they had been a part of inflicting, the pain which he had borne and which he continues to bear. And in that encounter with painful reality they discovered a deep joy; and in that same encounter he could wish them peace.

It is when we understand the pain which Christ bears and transforms through his resurrection, when we admit the harsh reality of the world in which we live, that we see the depths of what God's peace might mean. Understanding how great the need is can also be daunting, leaving us feeling hopeless: 'Nothing I may do can possibly make any difference.' And yet are we not called to transcend what is possible in the encounter with the risen Christ? 'Small actions of peace can become a cornerstone of peacemaking,' writes Reiko Shimado.[4] In the face of the harsh reality of the fallen world, even one small step towards a just peace may bring a glimpse of the living God to a person in despair, in grief, bowed down under injustice. An awareness of all that we cannot do is no reason not to do what we can.

When we see the next small step that we can take, we may also begin to understand the truth, not only of the pain of the world, but of how we have been gifted by God. Dietrich Bonhoeffer, writing his vision for 'Life Together' in the face of the Third Reich, puts it like this:

> We prevent God from giving us the great spiritual gifts he has in store for us, because we do not give thanks for daily gifts. We think we dare not be satisfied with the small measure of spiritual knowledge, experience and love that has been given to us, and that we must constantly be looking forward eagerly for the highest good. We deplore that fact that we lack the deep certainty, the strong faith and the rich experience that God has given to others, and we consider this lament to be pious. ... [But] how can God entrust great things to anyone who will not thankfully receive little things? If we do not give thanks daily for the Christian fellowship in which we have been placed, even where there is no great experience, no discoverable riches, but much weakness, small faith and difficulty; if on the contrary we only keep complaining to God that everything is so paltry and petty, so far from what we expected, then we hinder God from letting our fellowship grow according to the measure and riches which are there for us all in Jesus Christ.[5]

Our encounter with the risen Christ cannot take place if we pretend that things are other than they are. It is as ourselves that we are called to meet the risen Christ, as ourselves, and as part of the realities of the world which is God's world.

Christ's call to peace calls us to wage peace; that is, to invest into our active struggle for peace the energy we often use for war. This is a call to the painful realisation that our peace, our comfort, our security are all too often bought at the cost of the suffering of others, and to the hopeless admission of how little we can do. And yet, it is in the encounter with Christ that the realisation of our smallness is transformed into the joy and strength of understanding our own calling to be a part of God's transformation of the world. It is in that encounter that our despair is illuminated by the hope that the little we can do may indeed make a difference. The paradox is that it is precisely in and through the appalling realisation that there is no peace, that we are called into peace.

This is the peace of Christ into which we are invited. Not a false peace, which cries, 'Peace, Peace' when there is no peace, but the peace which comes when we understand that there is no peace and yet still seek to transform the world and live the peace of God, in God's justice and God's truth.

> We light this candle for peace, Lord.
> May its light scatter the darkness;
> may its flame be a symbol of hope;
> may its burning be a sign of faith
> joining with many other lights for peace.
> We light this candle for peace.
> May our lives be
> an expression of peace-making;
> may we seek to be lights in a dark world,
> pointing to you, Jesus,
> the Prince of Peace,
> and following you in the way of peace.
> Let the candle burn, as a sign for peace,
> offered to you.[6]

18

Another goodbye –
Ascension

Then [Jesus] said to them, 'These are my words that I spoke to you while I was still with you – that everything written about me in the law of Moses, the prophets, and the psalms must be fulfilled.' Then he opened their minds to understand the scriptures, and he said to them, 'Thus it is written, that the Messiah is to suffer and to rise from the dead on the third day, and that repentance and forgiveness of sins is to be proclaimed in his name to all nations, beginning from Jerusalem. You are witnesses of these things. And see, I am sending upon you what my Father promised; so stay here in the city until you have been clothed with power from on high.'

Then he led them out as far as Bethany, and, lifting up his hands, he blessed them. While he was blessing them, he withdrew from them and was carried up into heaven. And they worshipped him, and returned to Jerusalem with great joy; and they were continually in the temple blessing God.

Luke 24.44-53

When I think about the Ascension, I have a picture in my mind. I am not sure whether it is a painting or picture which really exists anywhere. In my mind I have this picture of Jesus disappearing into a cloud, with only his feet sticking out at the bottom, while all the disciples stand in a circle, gazing up to heaven, with their mouths open, quite astonished, rather afraid, looking what in Derbyshire would be called 'gob-smacked'. Whether or not this picture really exists as a painting, for me it is very vivid. And the thing that strikes me in it is not so much Jesus' feet sticking out of the cloud, but the faces of the disciples – astonished, confused, amazed, afraid. After all the strangeness of these post-Easter weeks, after the resurrection appearances and the encounters with Jesus the Christ who has died but is risen, after all that, the disciples (in Luke's Gospel at least) are faced with Jesus' being whisked away into heaven, with a parting which this time seems to be final. No wonder they are confused; no wonder they are astonished and taken aback and afraid. Here they are; they have just got used to the idea that Christ is with them after all, and off he goes again. Confused? I should think so. We might expect them to be confused, to be scared and anxious, to be sad and upset. Whatever else the Ascension is about, it seems that it is about saying a final farewell, about marking the end of Jesus' earthly ministry.

But if the Ascension *is* about saying farewell, then what happens next is very odd. The disciples do not settle down to mourn; they do not seem to be sad; they do not even try to return to normal daily life, as they did after the crucifixion. Not at all. Instead, Luke tells us, 'they returned to Jerusalem with great joy; and they were continually in the temple blessing God'. This doesn't seem quite the normal reaction to losing one's friend and leader, or what we might expect when someone who has been a close and integral part of the group is no longer there. How can they praise God, when they have just finally lost Jesus? How can they go back to Jerusalem, to the Temple, in joy and praise and worship?

I think it is possible because the 40 days of Easter, the 40 days of encounters with the risen Christ have changed the disciples' perspective, and with it the way in which they understand their future. This farewell is different from the last. The crucifixion had a finality which stopped the disciples dead in their tracks. It apparently had no future. But now the future has been opened up. The 40 days of strange, unexpected, and yet everyday encounters with Jesus have convinced the disciples that he is still present. And those 40 days have shifted their focus away from themselves, a group of frightened disciples, to the people who have been charged with a message. Jesus' promise to the disciples, 'I am sending upon you what my Father promised; be clothed with the power from on high', looks forward to Pentecost. It promises support for a task, the shared task of carrying the message of Jesus Christ to the nations, to proclaim repentance and forgiveness of sins. There has been a shift during these 40 days which comes into focus at Ascension and in the time that follows. The disciples' joy reflects not a suppression of emotion but the wonderful realisation that somehow, in a new and different way, Jesus' strength, his gifts and his inspiration, his life and his presence are still there, will be in their mouths and their hearts, will accompany them to the end of time, to the end of the age (Matthew 28.20). It is this shift which will allow the disciples to accept the gift of the Spirit at Pentecost, and to be strengthened for the task to come.

Rowan Williams has written of the Ascension in terms of the recognition that we should be looking, not at Jesus, but at the world. When we turn on a light in a room, we do not generally do so in order to look at the light-bulb, he suggests. We turn on the light to illumine the room, so that by that light we can see and act. Similarly, at the Ascension, as the light of Christ, a light which drew the eye to it, leaves the world, we are called to be the light, not so that others will look at us, but so that others can see the world in the light of Christ.[1] In his poem 'Kingfishers catch fire', Gerard Manley Hopkins describes the kind of person of whom this is not true, because they are persons focused on themselves: '*myself* it speaks and spells, / Crying *Whát I dó is me: for that I came*.'[2] Such people, suggests Hopkins (if I have understood him rightly), are like the kingfishers and dragonflies that catch fire, and draw flame, calling attention to themselves. But it is not enough to catch fire, to draw flame, to call attention to ourselves. What we do, what we say, what we live, must point beyond. 'The just man justices,' says Hopkins. Only the person who does justice, acts justly, is just. This is no abstract quality. The mother mothers; the father fathers; the lovers love; a relationship relates two people. The Christian lives Christ; the woman of grace 'keeps all [her] goings graces'. Of course we are ourselves, we can only be God's people, each of us, by being the individual person that God calls each of us to be. But we are called as ourselves to allow the light of God to flow through us and to illumine the world with God's light.

Living for Christ and not for the self is an ideal which is impossible to live up to, especially when we stop to think about it. All that we can really do is to realise that we live out who we are in our daily encounters, in our lives with one another. Through what we do, who we are, we bring joy – and, it must be said, sometimes grief – to those amongst whom and with whom we live. Through what we do, who we are, we shape their lives, just as they shape ours. Through who we are and how we live we become part of each other's lives, part of the rich tapestry which is God's world. Through living, we become who we are before God: through acting justly, through being honest, through waging peace, through mothering, loving, fathering, befriending. When we do all that with our minds on the other and not drawing attention to ourselves, we do it in Christ and for Christ. Through our 'being as communion', as John Zizioulas puts it,[3] through the way we are with one another, we help Christ to be seen in the world. For we are the Body of Christ as it now lives in the world. We incarnate the risen, ascended Christ to the world, and in our focus on Christ, we bring the world before him, before God. Ascension, suggests Christopher Irvine, summons Christians 'to raise their sights above daily preoccupations, to see the whole picture, and then to regard everything else in its light'.[4] To look up and see that in ascending to God's right hand, the material world – and with it ourselves – has also been redeemed and glorified.

But not for itself. And not for ourselves. 'As kingfishers catch fire, dragonflies draw flame;' writes Gerard Manley Hopkins. So, too, we must catch fire and draw flame, but to direct the eye of the beholder beyond ourselves, to act in God's eyes what in God's eyes we are. With the disciples between Ascension and Pentecost we must shift the focus away from ourselves to God, to God's world, to our task and calling in God's world, bringing the world before God. And it is, I believe, in our fulfilment of that task and calling, however incomplete, in our seeking to serve God in the world, to live out God's love, that we become most truly alive to the presence, not only of God, but of God in all those whose gifts have shaped – and continue to shape – our lives.

There is a very old legend, and all legends that persist speak truth, concerning the return of the Lord Jesus Christ to heaven after his ascension. It is said that the angel Gabriel met him at the gate. 'Lord, this is a great salvation that thou hast wrought,' said the angel. But the Lord Jesus only said, 'Yes.'

'What plans has thou made for carrying on the work? How are all to know what thou hast done?' asked Gabriel.

'I left Peter and James and John and Martha and Mary to tell their friends, and their friends to tell their friends, till all the world should know.'

'But Lord Jesus,' said Gabriel, suppose Peter is too busy with the nets, or Martha with the housework, or the friends they tell are too occupied, or forget to tell their friends – what then?'

The Lord Jesus did not answer at once; then he said in his quiet, wonderful voice: 'I have not made any other plans. I am counting on them.'[5]

19

Waiting and listening – the sixth week of Easter

Then they returned to Jerusalem from the mount called Olivet, which is near Jerusalem, a sabbath day's journey away. When they had entered the city, they went to the room upstairs where they were staying. Peter, and John, and James, and Andrew, Philip and Thomas, Bartholomew and Matthew, James son of Alphaeus, and Simon the Zealot, and Judas son of James. All these were constantly devoting themselves to prayer, including Mary the mother of Jesus, as well as his brothers.

Acts 1.12-14

The disciples let go of their encounter with the risen Christ, who was now ascended; and they waited. Perhaps this time they believed the promise, that they would be sent another guide. And so they had to wait; not to rush on to the next thing, but to wait.

Waiting is often not something that we take to kindly. I know I am impatient, and I hate queues, waiting at the checkout, sitting in traffic jams. But there are times when it is simply necessary to wait. One of my colleagues once said that the hardest part of childbirth for her was having to wait; being told by the midwife not to push. She likened those phases of not pushing – waiting – in labour to waiting on God, waiting on the Spirit. Waiting and listening.

When we seek God, it is important that we make space to wait and to listen. In the end, that means that it is important that we make time to pray, because prayer is as much about listening as about speaking. Even between people, communication is as much about listening (and even about watching) as about speaking. It is easy to forget that; I once asked a confirmation group to brainstorm associations with communication. They came up with all sorts of ideas but they were all to do with the voice or the gestures that someone was making. That is, they were all to do with the input into the process. But what about reception? Communication is not communication unless it is received. It is in the reception that the meaning comes into being. No communication can happen without two parties. Conversations need a listener as well as a speaker. Books need a reader as well as an author. Plays need an audience as well as a cast. Sermons need a congregation as well as a preacher. We need, all of us, to listen.

And so it is, too, with God. Jeremiah makes that point dramatically: 'For thus says the LORD of hosts, the God of Israel: Do not let the prophets and the diviners who are among you deceive you, and do not listen to the dreams that they dream, for it is a lie that they are prophesying to you in my name' (Jeremiah 29.8). Don't listen to them, or to me, listen to God!

When we listen, we may find ourselves hearing God's voice in many different places. Sometimes we hear it in the places we expect: at Bible study, or in the words of preachers or teachers, or at church. But we may find that all we hear in these places is spiritual gobbledegook, a sort of liturgical or theological white noise. Sometimes, we may have to distance ourselves from where we expect to hear God's word, step back from those who think they know, let go of those who think that they have God's word for us, who want to tell us what to do with our lives. Because God's voice is not always the one which shouts loudest, which is found in the books with the biggest circulation, in the most crowded places, or even the most dramatic events. God's voice can speak very quietly, in unexpected places, when we are least expecting it.

The story of Elijah includes a poignant reminder of this. Elijah is sitting in a cave waiting for the word of God:

> Now there was a great wind, so strong that it was splitting mountains and breaking rocks in pieces before the LORD, but the LORD was not in the wind; and after the wind an earthquake, but the LORD was not in the earthquake; and after the earthquake a fire, but the LORD was not in the fire; and after the fire a sound of sheer silence.
>
> 1 Kings 19.11b-12

'A sound of sheer silence'. The Authorised Version calls it 'a still small voice'. John Whittier's hymn is a reminder that hearing this still small voice can be deeply healing:

> Drop thy still dews of quietness, / till all our strivings cease; / take from our souls the strain and stress, / and let our ordered lives confess / the beauty of thy peace. / Breathe through the heats of our desire / thy coolness and thy balm; / let sense be dumb, let flesh retire; / speak through the earthquake, wind and fire, / O still small voice of calm.[1]

Hearing God, listening to God, being healed, may be very much a matter of coming to peace, of entering into silence, of allowing that still small voice to speak. And this is prayer. For prayer is for the most part listening and watchfully waiting, as Ann Lewin describes:

Prayer is like watching for the
Kingfisher. All you can do is
Be where he is likely to appear, and
Wait.
Often, nothing much happens;
There is space, silence and
Expectancy.
No visible sign, only the
Knowledge that he's been there,
And may come again.
Seeing or not seeing cease to matter.
You have been prepared.
But sometimes, when you've almost
Stopped expecting it,
A flash of brightness
Gives encouragement.[2]

For many of us God's presence is like this: like the presence of the kingfisher which was there a moment ago but is now gone, a glimpse, something that is nearly caught and yet not quite. A vision dreamed and vanished with the waking day. An emptiness. A silence. A hope. A waiting. God's presence is often not very tangible. But God is there. That is faith: as we wait, God is with us; in our doubts as well as our convictions; in our barrenness as well as in our fruitfulness; in our emptiness as well as our plenitude; in our silence as well as our words. And sometimes it is being barren which brings fruit, emptiness which brings plenty, silence that speaks.

It's not always easy to hear God's voice. In order to listen to God, we need to find stillness, and that may not be easy in the hectic round of our lives. In a world which is filled with background music and noise, we are not used to silence; we may find it unsettling; and we may well have to learn both to make and to bear it. 'Silence frees us from the need to control others,' writes Richard Foster. 'We are accustomed to relying upon words to manage and control others. ... We devour people with our words. Silence is one of the deepest disciplines of the Spirit simply because it puts a stopper on that.'[3] Silence slows us down; its texture takes us deeper than we may otherwise ever go. The American poet Kathleen Norris describes her experiences of 'making silence' with groups of school children:[4]

> I'll make a deal with you, I said – first you get to make noise, and then you'll make silence. ... The rules for silence were simple. Don't hold your breath and make funny faces ... Just breathe normally but quietly: the only hard thing is to sit so still that you make no noise at all. ... In every case but one, over many years, I found that children were able to become so still that silence became a presence in the classroom.

> Some kids loved it. I believe it was a revelation to them, and certainly to their teachers, that they could be so quiet. 'Let's do it again,' they'd say. Others weren't so sure. 'It's scary,' a fifth grader complained. 'Why?' I asked, and I believe that he got to the heart of it when he replied, 'It's like waiting for something – it's scary!'

Norris writes that the only class that couldn't make silence 'had so many little rules barked at them all day long by a burned-out teacher that they had stopped listening' – and listening is a prerequisite for hearing silence. But what really fascinated her was the way silence touched the children's imaginations and inspired them to deep imagery. She had them write about silence. 'Strength,' one child wrote, 'is as slow and silent as a tree.' 'Silence is spiders spinning their webs, it's like a silkworm making its silk.' 'Silence reminds me to take my soul with me wherever I go.' 'Lord, help me to know when to be silent.'

What do we hear when we make silence? What do we hear in those moments when the ascended Christ is no longer there, whilst we wait attentively for the coming of the Holy Spirit? Can we bear what we hear? We may not understand what we encounter there at all. 'Be still, and know that I am God!' says the Psalm (Psalm 46.10a). We cannot structure the knowledge of God; we can only seek it, be open to it, drink it into our souls. I come back over and over again to Eliot, to the *Four Quartets*, to the stillness of his waiting soul:

> I said to my soul, be still,
>   and wait without hope
> For hope would be hope of the wrong thing;
>   wait without love
> For love would be love of the wrong thing;
>   there is yet faith
> But the faith and the love and the hope are all
>   in the waiting.
> Wait without thought,
>   for you are not ready for thought:
> So the darkness shall be the light,
>   and the stillness the dancing.[5]

We may have to teach ourselves to make silence. We may have to learn to listen, to follow a sound into silence, as the Buddhists do, to go where the fading tone of the gong takes us into the arms of God, to stay with the pianissimo as it fades into eternity. When we do, when we let go of our busy-ness and our words and wait on God, God will be there.

'Silence reminds me to take my soul with me wherever I go.'

'Lord, help me to know when to be silent.'

'Be still and know that I am God.'

20

The Spirit of freedom and truth – Pentecost

When the day of Pentecost had come, they were all together in one place. And suddenly from heaven there came a sound like the rush of a violent wind, and it filled the entire house where they were sitting. Divided tongues, as of fire, appeared among them, and a tongue rested on each of them. All of them were filled with the Holy Spirit and began to speak in other languages, as the Spirit gave them ability. Now there were devout Jews from every nation under heaven living in Jerusalem. And at this sound the crowd gathered and was bewildered, because each one heard them speaking in the native language of each. Amazed and astonished, they asked, 'Are not all these who are speaking Galileans? And how is it that we hear, each of us, in our own native language? Parthians, Medes, Elamites, and residents of Mesopotamia, Judea and Cappadocia, Pontus and Asia, Phrygia and Pamphylia, Egypt and the parts of Libya belonging to Cyrene, and visitors from Rome, both Jews and proselytes, Cretans and Arabs – in our own languages we hear them speaking about God's deeds of power.' All were amazed and perplexed, saying to one another, 'What does this mean?' But others sneered and said, 'They are filled with new wine.'

But Peter, standing with the eleven, raised his voice and addressed them: 'Men of Judea and all who live in Jerusalem, let this be known to you, and listen to what I say. Indeed, these are not drunk, as you suppose, for it is only nine o'clock in the morning. No, this is what was spoken through the prophet Joel: "In the last days it will be, God declares, that I will pour out my Spirit upon all flesh, and your sons and your daughters shall prophesy, and your young men shall see visions, and your old men shall dream dreams. Even upon my slaves, both men and women, in those days I will pour out my Spirit; and they shall prophesy." '

Acts 2.1-18

Pentecost is the day that we celebrate the coming of the Holy Spirit. The Spirit which came, as it is described in Acts, like a rushing wind, a flickering tongue of fire, which sent those gathered together out into the streets to the crowd, to tell them what was happening. This is the Spirit which made them so excited that people thought that they must have had too much to drink – at nine o'clock in the morning. This is the Spirit which calls us to move as well: to act, to take courage, to live the heights and the depths of the life that God gives us: to pray, to weep, to sing, to grieve, to be angry, to laugh. To confess. To challenge. To change, ourselves and the world we live in.

The story of Pentecost begins with the disciples on their own in a room, shut up alone, in their tight-knit group. The Spirit comes, and suddenly they are on the street amongst the people gathered from throughout the world, shouting about what God had done. The Spirit has turned them, opened them out of themselves, shifted their focus from the group of those who know, and sent them into the world, to those who are to be told. 'Pentecost signifies freedom,' writes Bill Wylie Kellermann. 'Freedom now. Public freedom. Freedom from fear. ... The question to which Pentecost comes as a bold answer is this: Will the movement be ruled by fear? Will they be contained and confined? Rendered timid and silent? Pentecost says no.'[1] Pentecost calls us into the freedom of God.

This is glorious, but it is also hard, because freedom is a gift which we often do not know how to use well. 'Freedom is not easy, as its enemies and slanderers allege,' writes the philosopher Nicolas Berdyaev; 'Freedom is hard; it is a heavy burden.' In Berdyaev's thinking about freedom, there is a deep paradox: 'God desired freedom and freedom gave rise to tragedy in the world.'[2] Freedom is a gift of God, and yet freedom increases the suffering of the world. God gives us the gift of freedom, of free will, and we misuse it. In God's grace we are free, writes Luther, free from the fear imposed by systems that tell us we must earn God's grace, our salvation, free from the fear of a God who asks of us more than we can give and then punishes us for our failure, free to fail and still to be accepted by God, because grace is given freely. We are free and yet says Luther, at the same time we are slaves, for, despite God's gift of freedom through grace, we remain trapped in patterns of destruction and sin.[3] God's grace sets us free, and gives us courage, tempering the certain knowledge that we will fail.

We need that courage, because the Spirit calls us to move beyond the narrowness of where we are into the wideness of God's truth. Earlier, I referred to Margaret Silf's account of watching a canal boat in a lock. Of course, there is truth to be found about the lock's dark, dank, enclosed space, she points out. We could study the stones in the walls, the weeds, algae and snails that live there; we might discuss the design of the gates or how wood rots underwater. But to focus on the lock is entirely to miss its purpose. The

lock is there to move the boat on.[4] The lock gates are
useless unless they let in that powerful rush of water
which could drown a child – or, indeed, an adult –
and which, when I was a child, terrified me. But it is
that overpowering rush of water which lifts the boat
up, which allows the gates to open and the boat to
continue the journey. The truth of the lock is
incomplete without the wider truth of the canal,
incomplete without the wider truth that boats are
designed to move through and out and on. A ship in a
harbour – or a lock – is safe; but that is not what
ships are for.

So it is, too, with our lives. The Spirit brings us the
gifts of God's freedom anew, and in doing so opens us
to the eternity of God's truth. The Spirit challenges us
to see where the rushing power of the water – of the
Spirit – is breaking through the gates of our existence
and moving us through and out and on. And the
Spirit challenges us to open the closed doors of the
rooms in which we find ourselves, move away from
the places where we are safe and secure, out into the
tempestuous masses of people in our world. There is
a risk in this, of course: risk of rejection, risk of
conflict. But this is the necessary conflict that opens
our eyes to freedom and truth. The South African
theologian, John de Gruchy, believes that Pentecost
calls all people to dream God's dream.[5] Inspired by
God's Spirit, those who are oppressed or hurting look
beyond the traps of their own situation, see the vision
of the 'new heaven and the new earth', dream of
something better. And not only dream, but are
strengthened to face persecution, and find ways to
turn their living nightmare into a 'lived dream, which
is no-one's nightmare because it promises hope and
life in a new way for all'. This vision is deeply
threatening to those who 'possess everything except
the ability to share with others', for it shows clearly

where our apparent freedoms are oppressive and hurtful, unjust; points to the places where God's freedom and truth require radical change.

The Spirit of freedom is not the spirit of disdain, tempting us with the seductive call of 'you may choose to do anything to suit yourself'. The call of freedom must be tempered by truth if the gift of freedom is not simply to lead to self-indulgence. And, at the same time, it is freedom that rescues truth from mere exactitude, precision, which so often slips into being legalism. It is freedom which inspires truth with vision. It is truth which rescues freedom from laziness. We need to submit ourselves to the Spirit of truth even as we rejoice in and with the Spirit of freedom.

The call of freedom and truth takes us beyond externals to what is beyond appearances, to what is really real. This is something much deeper than simply what is measurable, or what I can persuade you to believe. Truth in its deepest sense is much more than your listening to me and saying yes, yes (or no, no). Freedom in its deepest sense is much more than simply my choice. The depths of freedom and truth are found in the quest, the search, the pilgrimage which is bringing us closer to God. One of the definitions of truth in the *Oxford English Dictionary* is 'steadfast in allegiance'. Truth, being true to someone or something, is about making that person, that thing, your centre, making them one of the places you check up with, one of the measures for your own integrity, your own authenticity, and the touchstone for your choices. To be centred on Christ is to be filled with the Spirit of freedom and truth. And that is the truth that sets us free. As Henry Thoreau once wrote:

If a man does not keep pace with his companions, perhaps it is because he hears a different drummer. Let him step to the music which he hears, however measured or far away.[6]

The Spirit of freedom and truth calls us to affirm Christ's truth as the drumbeat to which we wish to measure our steps, and to affirm our freedom to march to it, even when its beat is different from the myriad other beats that we hear in our lives. And so the Spirit calls us out of falsehood and into truth, out of captivity and into freedom.

O Holy Spirit, whose presence is liberty, grant us that freedom of the Spirit which will not fear to tread in unknown ways, nor be held back by misgivings of ourselves and fear of others. Ever beckon us forward to the place of your will, which is also the place of your power, O ever-leading, ever-loving Lord. Amen.[7]

21

Continually discovering our calling – the time after

> The eleven disciples went to Galilee, to the mountain to which Jesus had directed them. When they saw him, they worshipped him; but some doubted. And Jesus came and said to them, 'All authority in heaven and on earth has been given to me. Go therefore and make disciples of all nations, baptizing them in the name of the Father and of the Son and of the Holy Spirit, and teaching them to obey everything that I have commanded you. And remember, I am with you always, to the end of the age.
>
> Matthew 28.16-20

Jesus' great commission to the disciples brings us back to where we began: to our baptism. Our baptism is what appoints and calls us – each of us – to our ministry. When we hear the word 'ministry' we tend often to associate it with ordained ministry. But that is to mistake and to narrow the meaning of the word. The Church, the Body of Christ, exists in the world in the form of the presence of all the baptised, and ministry is the task shared by all the baptised, not the perquisite of the ordained. When I was preparing a group of young people for confirmation a few years ago, the group asked the Suffragan Bishop, who was then Henry Scriven, to write a letter about how he understood confirmation. The bishop wrote that confirmation is like a mini-ordination, which fills the candidate with the Holy Spirit and the strength and inspiration to do what God calls them to do, to go the ways in which God leads them. And this is true of baptism also: 'You are a chosen race, a royal priesthood, a holy nation, God's own people, in order that you may proclaim the mighty acts of him who called you out of darkness into his marvellous light' (1 Peter 2.9). Drawing on 1 Peter, Martin Luther taught that through baptism each of us is marked not only as belonging to the Church, but as one of that royal priesthood which is made up of all believers. Baptism is not primarily a mark of membership, but a call to proclamation, to witness to God's marvellous work of redemption.

Baptism, then, is the sacrament that points Christians to their true identity, their true character and their true calling. Discovering the nature of our calling, our ministry is therefore an essential part of our life in baptism. It is vitally important because when we discover our true calling, what it is that we have to offer as the unique person that God has created us to be, then we embark on the living of eternal life. That discovery may take time; we will try things out, take wrong roads, find ourselves on diversions or facing the blank end of a cul-de-sac. And it may be through trying things out that we discover what God wants of us.

There is a story about an acrobat who became tired of his life as a roving entertainer, always on the road, and joined the monastery at Clairvaux. But there he found that the words of the monks' prayers were in his mouth not true prayer, and so he went about his business silently, and when he saw others who seemed to know how to pray, he was ashamed. 'I am the only one to know nothing,' he thought to himself, and became sad and despairing.

'What am I doing here?' he asked himself. 'I don't know how to pray and cannot say a word. I am useless here and not worth the habit they have dressed me in.'

One day, when he heard the bells summoning the brothers to prayer, he was filled with grief and fled into a lonely chapel. 'If I cannot pray with the other monks,' he said to himself, 'I will at least do what I can.' He stripped off his habit and stood there in his colourful acrobat's costume. And he began to dance with his heart and his soul, springing forwards and back, to the left and to the right. He walked on his hands; he turned somersaults in the air. He danced his wildest, most extravagant dances in praise of God.

But one of the other monks had followed him. Through the chapel window, the monk watched the acrobat dancing and leaping, and fetched the abbot. A few days later, the abbot called the acrobat to him. The acrobat was terribly afraid and thought that he was to be punished for missing divine office.

He fell on the ground before the abbot and said, 'I know, father, that this is not the right place for me. And so I will go of my own free will and patiently endure the restlessness of life on the road.' But the abbot knelt before him, kissed him and lifted him up. Then he asked the acrobat to intercede for himself and for all the other monks: 'In your dancing you have praised God with your body and your soul. That is your prayer, for it comes from the depths of your heart. May God forgive all of us the easy words which cross our lips but are not echoed in our hearts.'[1]

We exercise our ministry most powerfully when we are able to serve God with our whole hearts, and to offer ourselves in freedom and in truth. We need not be continually exercised about what we have to offer, because God has made us, created us as our unique selves, made in God's image, and given us all that we need to praise and to serve.

This freedom can be difficult to grasp, because we are socialised to want 'to get it right'. Being set free to find God as God calls me can be terrifying. It can be much easier to follow rules and hold on to the comfort that by obeying them I must be believing right and so on the way to God. Being called to find God as God calls me can also be enormously liberating, an experience of true freedom. It can be an enormous relief to discover, as the acrobat did, that I do not have to seek God in the way that someone else has laid down for me, in the way that works for them. God invites us to approach, not by doing things in a particular way, not by being educated and seeking to understand everything, but like little children, open to accepting what we are given, what comes to us, in love and in joy, in wonder and openness. It is not that questioning or criticism or seeking perfection are outlawed. But there comes a point at which acceptance and not yet more questions, joy and not criticism, love, and not analysis, are the order of the day, for it is here that we find the trust and the courage to accept life – the whole of life, as we move again and again through the cycle from Ash Wednesday to Good Friday to Easter to Ascension to Pentecost, and on that way come to a better understanding that faith is not about getting something right, but about learning to know and to serve God.

This runs counter to the values of our achievement-oriented, competitive society, which so easily allows faith to be turned into a kind of spiritual competition. Great spiritual challenges can be seductive, because they can make us feel good about ourselves and our relationship with God. But they quickly become an end in themselves, focused on being demonstratively holy, which shifts the focus of our spiritual life away from God to ourselves. And they become addictive: to be right with God, I must do better and better; I must do more and more. This, as Martin Luther came to realise all too well, is a mistake; for when we set ourselves spiritual challenges, or expect God to set them, the mountain of works and achievements which must be scaled grows and grows and grows, becoming more and more daunting until in the end, like the acrobat when he was trying to pray as the monks did, we feel more and more inadequate, further and further from God. And yet it can also be a necessary mistake, for it is in the appalling realisation that our attempts to succeed have taken us far from God that we truly grasp that we cannot make ourselves holy, or perfect. Only God can do that. This is when we come to a true realisation that we cannot earn salvation, that nothing we can do will gain us the gift of God's grace. All that we can do is to have faith that we are accepted by God, and that although we are far away and do not deserve it, God reaches out to us and draws us in: 'When we were still far off, You met us in Your Son and brought us home.'[2]

This is the paradox of faith: that we are, as Luther said, *simul iustus et peccator*, at the same time sinner and saved. As we have moved through the cycle from Ash Wednesday to Pentecost, we have seen the depths to which sin can bring us, experienced the lonely distance we can be from God, and we have seen how that sin is forgiven, how that distance becomes intimacy when the risen Christ meets us where we are and the transforming power of the Holy Spirit is set free to work in our lives. But still in this world, in our lives, those encounters do not leave us finally saved, cleansed and shriven. As we obey the

great commission, as we respond to the call of our
baptism, we do so as people who are – at one and the
same time – broken and sinful; at the same time far
from God yet filled with God's grace. In our response
to the call of our baptism, we hold together in our
very being the fact that we are at one and the same
time Lenten, Good Friday people; and Easter,
Pentecost people, sent out by Christ to proclaim him
in the realities of God's world: 'Go therefore and
make disciples of all nations. ... And remember, I am
with you always, to the end of the age.'

O God, hear our prayer which we offer for all
your faithful people: that in our vocation and
ministry we may be equipped by the Spirit's
gifts to live out the gospel of Christ, in holiness
and truth, to the glory of your name. Amen.[3]

Let us go in peace to love and serve the Lord.
Thanks be to God.

Notes

Inspire gratefully acknowledges the use of copyright items. Every effort has been made to trace copyright owners, but where we have been unsuccessful we would welcome information which would enable us to make appropriate acknowledgement in any reprint.

Chapter 1
1. John Bell, *Church Times*, Easter 2003.
2. Rowan Williams, *Open to Judgement: Sermons and Addresses*, Darton, Longman & Todd, London, 1994, p. 119.
3. Rowan Williams, *Open to Judgement*, p. 97.

Chapter 2
1. Robert Frost, 'The Road Not Taken,' in *The Norton Anthology of Modern Poetry*, Norton, New York, 1973, p. 196.
2. James Alison, *On being liked*, Darton, Longman & Todd, London, 2003, p. 14.
3. Collect for the weekdays of the second week of Lent, *Die Feier der Eucharistie im Katholischen Bistum der Alt-Katholiken in Deutschland* (*Celebration of the Eucharist in the Old Catholic Diocese of Germany*), Bremberger Verlag, Munich 1995, p. 29 (translation CM).

Chapter 3
1. Cited by Karen Armstrong, 'Creativity cannot be hurried' in *The Guardian*, 24 April 2004.
2. Maggie Ross, *The Fire of Your Life: A Solitude Shared*, Darton, Longman & Todd, London, 1992, p. 25.
3. Wynes Simsic, *Pray without Ceasing: Mindfulness of God in Daily Life*, St Mary's Press, Winona, MN, 2000, p. 79.

4. Horst Balz, Farewell Lecture, Ruhr-Universität Bochum, 15.2.2002.
5. Allessandro Pronzato, *Meditations on the Sand*, St Paul Publications, Slough, 1992, pp. 9-10.
6. W.B. Yeats, 'The Second Coming', in: *Collected Poems*, Papermac (Macmillan), London, 1982, p. 210-11.
7. Eugen Eckert, 'Meine enge Grenzen' (translation CM; sung to a melody by Winfried Heurich).

Chapter 4
1. Kathleen Norris, *Amazing Grace: A Vocabulary of Faith*, Riverhead Books: New York 1998, pp. 69-70.
2. Margaret Guenther, *Holy Listening: the Art of Spiritual Direction*, Darton, Longman & Todd, London 1993, p. 9.
3. C.S. Lewis, *The Voyage of the Dawn Treader*, Penguin, Harmondsworth, 1965, pp. 95-96.

Chapter 5
1. Collect for the 24th Sunday of Ordinary Time, *Die Feier der Eucharistie im Katholischen Bistum der Alt-Katholiken in Deutschland* (*Celebration of the Eucharist in the Old Catholic Diocese of Germany*), Bremberger Verlag, Munich 1995, p. 280 (translation CM).

Chapter 6
1. Margaret Silf, *Landmarks: An Ignatian Journey*, Darton, Longman & Todd, London, 1998, p. 58.
2. R.S. Thomas, 'The Belfry,' in *Selected Poems 1946-1968*, Bloodaxe Books, Newcastle upon Tyne, 1986, p. 90.
3. Sheila Cassidy, *Sharing the Darkness: The Spirituality of Caring*, Darton, Longman & Todd, London, 1998, p. 78.
4. R.S. Thomas, 'The Belfry'.

5. R.S. Thomas, 'The Belfry'.
6. Margaret Silf, *Landmarks*, pp. 61-62.

Chapter 7

1. Joan Puls OSF, *Every Bush is Burning*, WCC, Geneva, 1985, pp. 51-52.
2. Dietrich Bonhoeffer, *Nachfolge* (Dietrich Bonhoeffer, *Werke*, vol. 4), Kaiser Verlag, Munich, ²1994, p. 31 (translation CM).

Chapter 8

1. Sara Maitland, 'Sacrifice,' in *Angel and Me: Short Stories for Holy Week*, Mowbray, London, 1995, pp. 30-35; quote p. 35.
2. Martin Luther King, *Strength to Love*, Fount, Glasgow, 1977, p. 154
3. Rowan Williams, *Open to Judgement: Sermons and Addresses*, Darton, Longman & Todd, London, 1994, p. 64.

Chapter 9

1. Collect for Holy Week, *Die Feier der Eucharistie im Katholischen Bistum der Alt-Katholiken in Deutschland* (*Celebration of the Eucharist in the Old Catholic Diocese of Germany*), Bremberger Verlag, Munich 1995, p. 41 (translation CM).

Chapter 10

1. Sheila Cassidy, *Sharing the Darkness: The Spirituality of Caring*, Darton, Longman & Todd, London, 1998, p. 78-79.
2. John Bell, 'The Teachers,' in *He Was in the World. Meditations for Public Worship*, Wild Goose, Glasgow, 1995, pp. 15-17.

Chapter 12

1. Rowan Williams, *Resurrection: Interpreting the Easter Gospel*, Darton, Longman & Todd, London, 1982, p. 119.
2. Janet Morley, *All Desires Known*, SPCK, London, 1992, p. 14.

Chapter 13

1. *Church Times*, 20.4.00, p. 18.
2. Isabelle Stengers, 'Science and Religion: Beyond Complementarily?' in *Design and Disorder: Perspectives from Science and Theology*, ed. by Niels Henrik Gregersen and Ulf Görman, T. & T. Clark, Edinburgh, 2002, p. 126.
3. Kathy Keay, 'After Breast Cancer Diagnosis April 1993,' in: *Dancing on Mountains: An Anthology of Women's Spiritual Writings*, compiled by Kathy Keay and Rowena Edlin-White, HarperCollins, London, 1996, p. 127.
4. T.S. Eliot, 'The Four Quartets: Little Gidding,' I, in *The Complete Poems and Plays of T.S. Eliot*, Faber and Faber, London, 1969, p. 192.
5. Based on the Collect for Easter Monday, *Die Feier der Eucharistie im Katholischen Bistum der Alt-Katholiken in Deutschland* (*Celebration of the Eucharist in the Old Catholic Diocese of Germany*), Bremberger Verlag, Munich 1995, p. 83.

Chapter 15

1. Leonardo Boff, *Sacraments of Life; Life of the Sacraments*, Pastoral Press, Washington DC, 1987, p. 3.
2. Roy Campbell, 'Mass at Dawn' in Charles Causley (ed.), *The Sun, Dancing*, Puffin, Harmondsworth, 1984, p. 220.
3. Leonardo Boff, *Sacraments of Life; Life of the Sacraments*, p. 32.

4. Based on the Post-Communion Prayer for Easter Monday, *Die Feier der Eucharistie im Katholischen Bistum der Alt-Katholiken in Deutschland* (*Celebration of the Eucharist in the Old Catholic Diocese of Germany*), Bremberger Verlag, Munich 1995, p. 83.

Chapter 16
1. Elizabeth Barrett Browning, 'Sonnets from the Portuguese', number 43.
2. Summary of the law from *Common Worship*, Church House Publishing, London, 2000, p. 168. Compare Deuteronomy 6.4 and Matthew 22.37-39.
3. Sara Maitland, *Home Truths*, Hodder and Stoughton, London 1994, p. 228.
4. Walter Hermann Fritz, 'Liebesgedichte', number II, in: *Gesammelte Gedichte*, Hoffmann und Campe Verlag, Hamburg, 1979 (translation by CM). Copyright © 1979 by Hoffmann und Campe Verlag, Hamburg. Used with permission.

Chapter 17
1. Alfred Nolan, 'Taking Sides' in *Mennonite Meditation and Facilitation Manual*, p. 44.
2. Martin Luther King, *Strength to Love*, Fount, Glasgow, 1977, p. 150.
3. Cited in *Resources for Preaching and Worship: Year C*, compiled by Hannah Ward and Jennifer Wild, Westminster John Knox, Louisville, 2003, p.231.
4. Reiko Shimado, 'War and Peace: A Japanese Perspective,' in: *Justice as Mission: An Agenda for the Church*, ed. by Terry Brown and Christopher Lind, Trinity Press, Burlington, Ontario, 1985, pp. 225-26.
5. Dietrich Bonhoeffer, *Life Together*, SCM Press, London, 1963, p. 19.

6. John Johansen-Berg, in *The SPCK Book of Christian Prayer*, SPCK, London, 1995, p. 162.

Chapter 18

1. Rowan Williams, *Open to Judgement: Sermons and Addresses*, Darton, Longman & Todd, 1994, pp. 81-82.
2. Gerard Manley Hopkins, 'Kingfishers catch fire' in *Poems and Prose*, ed. by W. H. Gardner, Penguin, Harmondsworth, 1953, p. 51.
3. John Zizioulas, *Being as Communion: Studies in Personhood and the Church*, Darton, Longman & Todd, London, 1985.
4. Christopher Irvine, 'Spinning a Tale and Catching a Vision: Preaching on the Ascension' in *Celebrating the Easter Mystery: Worship Resources from Easter to Pentecost*, ed. Christopher Irvine, Mowbray, London 1996, p. 111.
5. Text © 1991 George MacLeod, compilation © Ronald Ferguson, from *Daily Readings with George MacLeod*, 2001, Wild Goose Publications, Glasgow G2 3DH, Scotland, www.ionabooks.com

Chapter 19

1. John Greenleaf Whittier, 'Dear Lord and Father of Mankind'.
2. Ann Lewin, *Watching for the Kingfisher*, Inspire, Peterborough, 2004, p. 29.
3. Richard Foster, *Freedom of Simplicity*, Triangle, London, 1981, pp. 57-58.
4. Kathleen Norris, *Amazing Grace: A Vocabulary of Faith*, Riverhead Books: New York 1998, pp. 16-17.
5. T.S. Eliot, 'The Four Quartets: East Coker,' III, in: *The Complete Poems and Plays of T.S. Eliot*, Faber and Faber, London, 1969, p. 180.

Chapter 20

1. Bill Wylie Kellermann, *Seasons of Faith and Conscience: Kairos, Confession, and Liturgy*, Orbis, Maryknoll NY, 1991, p. 200-1.
2. Nicolas Berdyaev, *Dream and Reality: An essay in autobiography*, Geoffrey Bles, London, 1950, p. 46.
3. Martin Luther, *Die Freiheit eines Christen-menschen*, 1520.
4. Margaret Silf, *Landmarks: An Ignatian Journey*, Darton, Longman & Todd, London, 1998, pp. 61-62.
5. John de Gruchy, 'One person's dream is another's nightmare' in *Cry Justice*, Collins, London, 1986, pp. 232-33.
6. Quoted in *In a Dark Time*, ed. by Nicholas Humphrey and Robert Jay Lifton, Faber and Faber, London, 1984, p. 131.
7. George Appleton, in *The Oxford Book of Prayer*, ed. by George Appleton, Oxford University Press, Oxford, 1985, p. 92.

Chapter 21

1. Hubertus Halbfas, 'Der betende Gaukler,' in *Der Sprung in den Brunnen. Eine Gebetsschule*, Patmos Verlag, Düsseldorf 1988 (translation CM), pp. 135-37.
2. Prayer after Communion, *Common Worship*, Church House Publishing, London, 2000, p. 182.
3. Based on Collects for the Fifth and the Twentieth Sundays after Trinity, *Common Worship*, pp. 410 and 420.